CULTURES OF THE WORLD
Côte d'Ivoire

Cavendish
Square
New York

Published in 2019 by Cavendish Square Publishing, LLC
243 5th Avenue, Suite 136, New York, NY 10016

Third Edition

Website: cavendishsq.com

This publication represents the opinions and views of the author based on his or her personal experience, knowledge, and research. The information in this book serves as a general guide only. The author and publisher have used their best efforts in preparing this book and disclaim liability rising directly or indirectly from the use and application of this book.

All websites were available and accurate when this book was sent to press.

Library of Congress Cataloging-in-Publication Data

Names: Sheehan, Patricia, 1954- author. | Ong, Jacqueline, 1983- author. | Duling, Kaitlyn, author.
Title: Cote d'Ivoire / Patricia Sheehan, Jacqueline Ong, and Kaitlyn Duling.
Description: Third edition. | New York : Cavendish Square, 2019. |
Series: Cultures of the world | Includes bibliographical references and index.
Identifiers: LCCN 2019000407 (print) | LCCN 2019002022 (ebook) |
ISBN 9781502647351 (ebook) | ISBN 9781502647344 (library bound)
Subjects: LCSH: Côte d'Ivoire--Juvenile literature.
Classification: LCC DT545.22 (ebook) | LCC DT545.22 .S54 2019 (print) |
DDC 966.68--dc23
LC record available at https://lccn.loc.gov/2019000407

Editorial Director: David McNamara
Editor: Kristen Susienka
Copy Editor: Nathan Heidelberger
Associate Art Director: Alan Sliwinski
Designer: Jessica Nevins
Production Coordinator: Karol Szymczuk
Photo Research: J8 Media

The photographs in this book are used by permission and through the courtesy of: Cover Walter Zerla/Cultura Exclusive/Getty Images; p. 1 Boulenger Xavier/Shutterstock.com; p. 3 Newphotoservice/Shutterstock.com; p. 5 N. Cirani/DeAgostini/Getty Images; p. 6, 23, 36, 39, 40, 46, 72, 76, 77, 78, 81, 87, 95, 97, 101, 104, 124, 127, 129 Issouf Sanogo/AFP/Getty Images; p. 10 Education Images/UIG/Getty Images; p. 12, 21, 29, 30, 33, 35, 38, 52, 62, 70, 79, 82, 86, 105, 106, 108, 112, 114, 118, 121, 122 Sia Kambou/AFP/Getty Images; p. 13 Dave Montreuil/Shutterstock.com; p. 14 Universal Images Group/Getty Images; p. 15 Cedric Favero/Moment/Getty Images; p.18 Prisma/UIG/Getty Images; p. 20 ZU 09/Digital Vision Vectors/Getty Images; p. 25 Rolls Press/Popperfoto/Getty Images; p. 28 Alvaro Canovas/Paris Match/Getty Images; p. 43 Michael Nagle/Bloomberg/Getty Images; p. 44 Mtcurado/iStock/Getty Images; p. 47 Archistoric/Alamy Stock Photo; p. 50, 74 Charles O. Cecil/Alamy Stock Photo; p. 53 Xinhua News Agency/Getty Images; p. 56, 66 L. Romano/DeAgostini/Getty Images; p. 59 Bruce Dale/National Geographic/Getty Images; p. 61 Jaccod/DeAgostini/Getty Images; p. 64 Fabian Plock/iStock/Getty Images; p. 84 Fabian Plock/iStockphoto.com; p. 90 Universal Images Group/Getty Images; p. 92 Jbdodane/Alamy Stock Photo; p. 96 Schalk van Zuydam/AP Images; p. 98 Peter Horree/Alamy Stock Photo; p. 102 Elena Dijour/Shutterstock.com; p. 107 MyLoupe/UIG/Getty Images; p. 110 Sa Terli/Anadolu Agency/Getty Images; p. 113 (top, bottom) Sia Kambou/AFP/Getty Images, Jean Catuffe/Getty Images; p. 116 Melba Photo Agency/Alamy Stock Photo; p. 119 C. Sappa/DeAgostini/Getty Images; p. 120 Thierry Gouegnon/Reuters/Newscom; p. 130 Serein/Wikimedia Commons/File:Kedjenou.JPG/CC BY SA 3.0; p. 131 Amallia Eka/Shutterstock.com.

Printed in the United States of America

CONTENTS

CÔTE D'IVOIRE TODAY   **5**

1. GEOGRAPHY

Land • National parks • Waterways • Climate zones • Plants • Animal life • Major cities   **9**

2. HISTORY

Clans • The slave trade • A French colony • A fight for freedom • Post-independence • Conflict • The first civil war • Temporary peace • Election and aftermath • Recent events   **19**

3. GOVERNMENT

Decentralization • Political structure • New constitution • Election issues • A history of distrust • Armed forces of Côte d'Ivoire • Freedoms • Human rights • Global reach   **31**

4. ECONOMY

Agricultural reliance • Debt and aid • Exports • Cocoa and coffee • Industry • Timber • Mining the earth • Tourists • Foreign trading • Money • Transportation and communication • Energy • Work   **45**

5. ENVIRONMENT

Forest depletion • Illegal logging • The Voluntary Partnership Agreement • Comoé National Park • 2006 toxic waste event   **57**

6. IVORIANS

Population • Many ethnic groups • Non-Ivorians • Economic inequality   **65**

7. LIFESTYLE

Family • Women • Education • Men • Character • Customs • Clothing • Events • Daily life • Cities • Rural life • Health   **73**

8. RELIGION Muslims • Muslim houses of worship • Christians • Christian houses of worship • Indigenous religion • Blending religions **85**

9. LANGUAGE Tone languages • National language • Telling stories • Sharing information **93**

10. ARTS History • Wearable art • Music and dance • Musical traditions • Contemporary music • Indigenous dance • Cloth • Writers **99**

11. LEISURE Games • Stories • Athletics • Having fun **111**

12. FESTIVALS Christian celebrations • Islamic holy days • Other traditions **117**

13. FOOD Mealtime • Ivorian specialties • Drinks • Restaurants • Buying food **123**

MAP OF CÔTE D'IVOIRE **133**

ABOUT THE ECONOMY **135**

ABOUT THE CULTURE **137**

TIMELINE **138**

GLOSSARY **140**

FOR FURTHER INFORMATION **141**

BIBLIOGRAPHY **142**

INDEX **143**

CÔTE D'IVOIRE TODAY

NESTLED ON THE WEST AFRICAN COAST BETWEEN FIVE OTHER nations and the Atlantic Ocean, the République de Côte d'Ivoire, also known as the Ivory Coast, has a long and storied past, a rich cultural history, and a hopeful vision for its future. The country received its name from French sailors who traded ivory along its coast. Like much of Africa, by 1893 Côte d'Ivoire had lost its independence to colonization. It was ruled from afar by the French. However, Côte d'Ivoire was unique among West African colonized areas in that the French lived in the region not only as bureaucrats but as settlers. French residents owned coffee, cocoa, and banana plantations that helped establish the country as one of the main exporters of coffee, cocoa, and palm oil, among other agricultural products.

Even after retaking independence in 1960, the country retained close ties with France, among other allies and economic partners, and it experienced early prosperity. Immigrants from the surrounding countries of Liberia, Guinea, Mali, Burkina Faso, and Ghana came to Côte d'Ivoire to work on farms, helping production expand to new levels. Immigrants continued to arrive from France as well, and the country grew both in population and economic wellness.

These soldiers stand guard in 2004. Armed men were a common sight in Côte d'Ivoire during years of civil unrest.

CHALLENGES

While growing economically, Côte d'Ivoire has not been immune to extensive periods of political unrest and even civil war. Several political leaders with strong personalities and ideas have gained and lost power over the years, and 1999 saw a military coup that sent a president into exile. Since that year, unrest, public uprisings, and violent protests have marred daily life across Côte d'Ivoire. From 2002 to 2004, the country was engaged in the First Ivorian Civil War, a battle between the Muslim northern rebels and a government-led group of Christians in the south. Neighboring countries, France, and the United Nations sent in troops to maintain boundaries, but the war continued unabated for over two years. A final peace accord between the rebels and the government didn't come until 2007, and by that time, infrastructure across the nation had been damaged. The country would need to rebuild.

The most recent outbreaks of violence in Côte d'Ivoire occurred in 2010, a result of political conflict after the 2010 presidential election. This period, known as the Second Ivorian Civil War, plagued the country until 2011. Now, once more, Côte d'Ivoire is in a state of rebuilding. Armed conflicts and tension continue to threaten peace at home, but those displaced by the election-related violence in 2010 have begun to return, and recent spurts of foreign investment are breathing new life into an economy long dominated by agricultural exports.

OPPORTUNITIES

Though the nation has been marked by passionate and violent disagreements between citizens, governments, and rebel groups, Côte d'Ivoire's diversity and rich cultural history offer some of the greatest opportunities for the country going forward. There are over sixty unique ethnic groups in the country, and many of them are affiliated with groups in bordering nations. While the official language is French, a variety of languages are spoken across different regions and groups, and religious affiliation remains mixed as well. Muslims, Christians, animists, and others make up a diverse range of believers. This mixed population has brought different holidays, rituals, and celebrations to the country, and varying houses of worship dot the urban and rural landscapes.

While tourism is not the main economic driver in the country, every year thousands of travelers check Côte d'Ivoire off their list of visited destinations. Known for its beautiful beaches, wildlife preserves, tourist-centric villages, and French colonial legacy, it has plenty to offer to visitors, especially during times of consistent peace. Though its resources have come under threat in the twentieth and twenty-first centuries, Côte d'Ivoire still contains vast, lush rain-forest preserves that offer hiking trails, wildlife, and beautiful views. The country's economic capital, Abidjan, is a coastal city and major urban center marked by skyscrapers, museums, and religious landmarks. Its governmental capital, Yamoussoukro, is home to government business but sees much less tourism.

Rapid growth has given Côte d'Ivoire a youthful and energetic personality, even amid political turbulence. Over half of the population is under twenty-five years of age, and the population continues to grow every year.

TOWARD A FUTURE

Both residents and witnesses to Côte d'Ivoire's many changes over the years are hopeful that the country is growing in its stability and sense of unity, which could lead to more peace and prosperity in the future. President Alassane Dramane Ouattara has been in place since 2010, and the economy is on pace to continue its growth and development. With a nation full of young minds and rich in resources, Côte d'Ivoire could see more prosperity in the coming decades.

GEOGRAPHY

Côte d'Ivoire's coastal beaches are warm and beautiful.

1

"Do not call the forest that shelters you a jungle."
—African proverb

ON THE SOUTHERN COAST OF WEST Africa, tucked between several other nations and bordering the Gulf of Guinea and the Atlantic Ocean, is Côte d'Ivoire. A nation of great diversity, it has many physical features—flat and sandy coastlines, tropical forests, and rocky mountains. With an area of 124,504 square miles (322,463 square kilometers), slightly larger than the state of New Mexico, the country shares its borders with Mali and Burkina Faso to the north, Liberia and Guinea to the west, and Ghana to the east. Its topography consists of coastal lowland, rain-forest plateau, and upland savanna. To really understand the country, one must visit its different regions, including vast rural areas and dense, lively cities. There is no singular Côte d'Ivoire. Its many flavors, stories, histories, and personalities are what make this country great.

LAND

The hot, dry savanna in Comoé National Park is peppered with elephants and other wildlife.

On the south of Côte d'Ivoire lies a 320-mile- (515-kilometer-) long strip of coastal land bordering the Gulf of Guinea. This seafront area is marked by a number of lagoons and sandy beaches.

The southeast and central regions are home to the Baule, Anyi, and Abron peoples. The lands around their farms contain the remnants of rain forests that once covered all of southern Côte d'Ivoire. Like much of the rest of West Africa, Côte d'Ivoire has suffered severe deforestation. Agriculture, uncontrolled fires, and logging for tropical woods have been the primary causes of forest loss. According to environmentalists, Côte d'Ivoire is at risk of losing *all* of its forest cover by 2034 if no changes are made and deforestation continues at its current rate.

In the north, the land changes to savanna—a large plateau consisting primarily of rolling hills, low-lying vegetation, and scattered trees. Compared with many parts of Africa, the arable land is mostly flat with relatively rich, sandy soil. Such terrain favors the growing of crops, mainly dry rice (rice not grown in flooded paddies), peanuts, and millet.

In the northwest are two mountainous regions, called the Odienné and Man, where several summits rise to more than 5,000 feet (1,524 meters). The highest peak, Mount Nimba, towers over them all at 5,748 feet (1,752 meters).

NATIONAL PARKS

Côte d'Ivoire is home to several national parks that preserve the country's beauty and wildlife.

COMOÉ NATIONAL PARK, also called the Komoé, 352 miles (566 km) from the city of Abidjan, is West Africa's largest game park. Tucked in the northeast corner of Côte d'Ivoire, it has an area of about 4,440 square miles (11,500 sq km) of savannas, forests, and grasslands. One of the most popular hunting trails during the dry season is along the Comoé (or Komoé) River, where most of the game gathers in search of water. Animals found in the park include elephants, lions, hippopotamuses, leopards, antelopes, colobus and green monkeys, and wild hogs. Over four hundred species of birds have been sighted there.

TAÏ NATIONAL PARK contains some of the last rain forests in West Africa. The park is about 1,274 square miles (3,300 sq km). Tall trees block out the sunlight, preventing dense undergrowth. This primary forest also consists of hanging tropical vines called lianas, torrential streams, and abundant original wildlife. The park is noted for its chimpanzees, which have been the subject of wildlife studies, as well as for its rare pygmy hippopotamuses.

WATERWAYS

There are four principal river systems, including the Sassandra, Bandama, Cavally, and Comoé. Each river is navigable for only about 40 miles (64 km) of its total length because during the dry season their water levels are extremely low, while during the rainy season it is nearly impossible to navigate through the rapids. The 1960s and 1970s saw the building of several dams to control river flow, which have created reservoirs or "lakes" across the country.

CLIMATE ZONES

Côte d'Ivoire has two distinct climatic zones. Along the coast, the weather is humid. Temperatures vary from 72 degrees Fahrenheit (22 degrees Celsius) to 90°F (32°C). In the northern savanna, temperature differences are more extreme. In the summer, temperatures can drop to 54°F (12°C) at night and rise above 104°F (40°C) in the day. The northern area has an average annual rainfall of 51 inches (130 centimeters), whereas the average annual rainfall in the southern region is 65 inches (165 cm). On the mountains in the west, rainfall totals 80 inches (203 cm). From early December to February, strong harmattan winds blow dust and desert sand from the Sahara, reducing visibility in the northern mountain regions. The country has three seasons—November to

Côte d'Ivoire is the sixty-eighth-largest country in the world in terms of land area.

Primates like this one call Taï National Park their home.

March is warm and dry; March to May is hot and dry; June to October is hot and wet. July is the wettest of all months.

PLANTS

The savanna is covered by low grasses, shrubs, and small deciduous trees. In this arid zone the unusual baobab tree survives by storing water in its trunk, which allows it to get through the dry season. The trunk of the baobab tree can grow to a diameter of 26 feet (8 m), and it can store as much as 31,701 gallons (120,000 liters) of water in its soft wood. In times of drought, the baobab trees are often scraped by elephants that break into the tree trunk to get at its water.

Central and southern Côte d'Ivoire is covered by tropical rain forests with more than 225 species of trees. This area of forest receives an average annual rainfall of more than 43 inches (110 cm). Evergreens and oil palms tower above its dense surface covering of shrubs, ferns, and mosses. There are numerous species of tropical hardwood trees, including obeche, mahogany, and iroko (African teak). This area is a great natural resource because the tropical hardwoods are such commercially prized assets.

ANIMAL LIFE

The animal life in Côte d'Ivoire is similar to that of its next-door neighbor Ghana. Characterized by a great variety of distinctive animals and birds, the country's wildlife is part of the Ethiopian biogeographic zone. Herds of elephants roam the woodlands and grasslands, which are also home to chimpanzees. Carnivores such as hyenas, jackals, and panthers live in the same region. There are large numbers of antelope and wild hogs in the country; the most plentiful hog is the red river hog. Manatees, herbivorous water mammals, also live in some rivers.

The longest and most commercially important river in Côte d'Ivoire is the Bandama. It is home to the country's largest dam. It is also where over one hundred species of freshwater fish live, contributing to the nation's fishing industry. The river houses the Kossou hydroelectric power plant, which produces electricity and provides an irrigation system. Completed in 1973, the plant was a key economic development for Côte d'Ivoire. It includes the artificial Lake Kossou, which the Bandama now flows through on its way to the Gulf of Guinea.

Most birdlife belongs to Eurasian groups. The guinea fowl is the main game bird. It lives in the forests, is covered with bluish-white spots, and has a red throat and a crest of curly black feathers. In the savanna, the blue-bellied roller bird, which has a green beak and feet, is common. The birds are easily spotted on bushes, where they search for insects.

Reptiles found in the country include lizards and crocodiles. Pythons and a variety of venomous snakes can also be found. There are many insects, notably mosquitoes, driver ants, termites, locusts, and tsetse flies.

A brilliant blue-bellied roller takes flight.

MAJOR CITIES

Côte d'Ivoire has many thriving cities. Each city offers a unique blend of individuals and experiences.

YAMOUSSOUKRO, also called the Radiant City, has a population of 231,000. It was designated the official capital by President Félix Houphouët-Boigny in 1983. Because of its central location, Yamoussoukro is easily accessible from all parts of the nation, and a high level of commercial activity occurs there. The city's economy is primarily dependent on the fishing, timber, and perfume

Deforestation is one of the biggest problems facing the country's environment today. The country was once primarily noted for its forest resources. Since the nation gained independence in 1960, however, the forested area has been cut from 29.6 million acres (12 million hectares) to 7.4 million acres (3 million ha). The loss of these rain forests has triggered many environmental problems that have contributed to social unrest and exacerbated poverty across the country. As such, rain-forest destruction is of national concern.

Deforestation increased over the years because of the expansion of the timber industry and agriculture. When coffee and cocoa prices fell in the 1980s, the country concentrated on exporting wood to Europe, its largest trading partner. The government imposed a ban on unprocessed timber exports in 1995, and reforestation began in numerous locations. However, illegal logging, accelerating after the start of the civil war in 2002 and continuing in the subsequent years, has contributed to the country's having one of the highest deforestation rates in the world. Millions of acres of tropical rain forest have also been destroyed to make room for cocoa and other commodity plantations. Since cacao trees, which produce the beans to make cocoa, deplete the soil's nutrients very quickly, plantation owners are driven time after time to clear virgin forest to take advantage of its fertile soil.

Steps are being taken to curb cocoa plantations, some of which have been set up in protected areas. In the spring of 2018, the government of Côte d'Ivoire took a few initial steps in partnership with cocoa farmers and chocolate makers to protect its national parks and reserves by halting the spread of cocoa plantations in those areas. Many major companies, including Mars and Hershey, pledged to stop sourcing cocoa from protected areas. However, about 40 percent of Côte d'Ivoire's cocoa was coming from protected areas as of 2018, and it will take some large-scale changes to make a difference. The change will affect the lives of farmers and their families and must be handled carefully.

The rate of deforestation is also greatly increased by subsistence farming methods practiced in the country. Destructive forest fires occur regularly because of extensive slash-and-burn practices, leaving too many openings in the forest cover.

The ultimate results of deforestation are the extinction of plants and animals, the loss of medicinal plants, an increase in mosquito-borne malaria, changes in rainfall patterns leading to infertile land, and radically altered rural living conditions.

industries, and the country's major export crops, cocoa and coffee, are grown near there. In addition, Yamoussoukro's economic fabric includes automobile trade and textiles. Yamoussoukro is also the site of the Basilica of Our Lady of Peace, claimed to be the world's largest church.

ABIDJAN was a small fishing village of about seven hundred inhabitants when it became the terminus of the railroad to the interior in 1904. Nevertheless, with no port facilities, growth was slow. In 1934, when Côte d'Ivoire was still a French colony, Abidjan became the capital. It retained this status even after independence because, by then, the French had finished building the Vridi Canal that connected Abidjan's lagoon to the ocean. This instantly gave the city an excellent harbor, and modern port operations commenced soon after. Today, Abidjan is Côte d'Ivoire's main port and largest city. It is the hub of the country's

Abidjan has grown from a small fishing village to a major destination city.

East of the bustling city of Abidjan lies a town that is slower, sandier, and often considered a getaway for both tourists and residents of Côte d'Ivoire. Grand-Bassam was the French colonial capital city from 1893 to 1896, and today it retains its rich colonial history and architecture. There are cathedrals, grand colonial buildings, and museums. In 2012, the coastal town earned the distinction of a UNESCO World Heritage Site. The town also features a long strip of white, sandy beach that is backed by beautiful palm orchards. It is a popular weekend escape for those who live in Abidjan during the week. It is not uncommon to see luxury hotels in various stages of construction along the coast in Grand-Bassam.

rail and road systems and the center of its cultural and commercial life. It is also home to the national university, several technical colleges, libraries, and an art museum. Even though Yamoussoukro was designated as the nation's capital, most government offices and foreign embassies are located in Abidjan.

Over the years, the population of Abidjan has climbed to 4.9 million people. Known as the Paris of West Africa, Abidjan has a large French population. It also attracts Africans from neighboring countries, making it the region's most cosmopolitan city. Abidjan in the twenty-first century is characterized by high industrialization and urbanization. It is an attractive and modern city, having skyscrapers—an uncommon sight in West Africa—as well as many parks and wide boulevards, inspired by the French.

BOUAKÉ is located in central Côte d'Ivoire, where the southern forests meet the savanna. It is the country's second-largest city. It was established as a French military post in the late 1890s and once had served as a major slave market. It is now an important administrative and commercial center. In addition, it is the central market for cocoa, coffee, cotton, yams, and other agricultural products harvested in the region. Bouaké is also the site of a school of forestry and a cotton-textile research institute, and it is renowned for its sprawling market and carnival.

Other urban centers include Man in the west, Korhogo in the north, Bondoukou in the east, and San-Pédro in the southwest. San-Pédro is a major port and a center for the exportation of timber and palm oil. It is about 40 miles (64 km) southwest of the famed Taï National Park.

With its mix of urban centers, swathes of forest, and sand beaches, Côte d'Ivoire boasts a diverse array of landscapes. In just a short drive or bus ride, one can travel from the top of a tall mountain to the sunny coast of the Gulf. Over the years, increased agriculture work has greatly threatened the country's rich rain forests, but efforts to end (or at least slow) deforestation have begun in earnest in the 2010s. As we move closer to the middle of the twenty-first century, it will be up to the local farmers, major corporations, and federal government to keep protected areas safe and curb any new deforestation projects. Only then will the gorgeous, biodiverse landscapes of Côte d'Ivoire remain for everyone to enjoy.

INTERNET LINKS

https://www.awf.org/region/westcentral-africa
You can explore the wildlife of West Africa on this page hosted by the African Wildlife Foundation.

https://forest500.org/rankings/jurisdictions/ivory-coast
The Forest 500 rankings on deforestation help give a complete picture of deforestation in the country.

https://www.nationalparks-worldwide.com/ivory_coast.htm
This is a comprehensive guide to the national parks and other protected areas of Côte d'Ivoire.

https://whc.unesco.org/en/list/227
This UNESCO site provides information on Comoé National Park in Côte d'Ivoire.

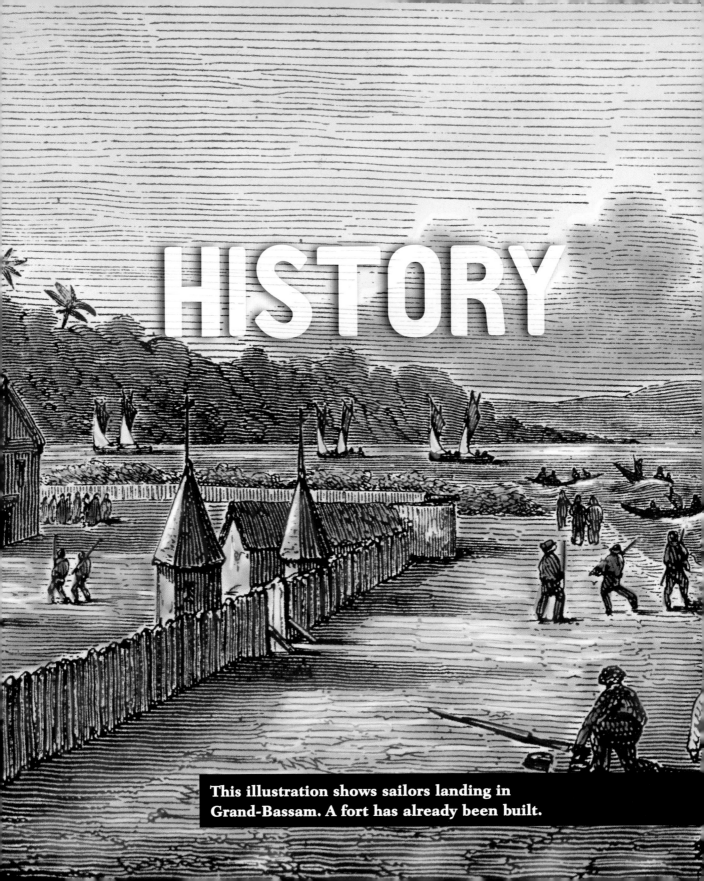

HISTORY

This illustration shows sailors landing in Grand-Bassam. A fort has already been built.

2

THE HISTORY OF CÔTE D'IVOIRE IS complex. From French colonial region to independent nation, the country has paraded through peacetimes and battled through civil wars. Political unrest and colonialism have created a large diasporic community in France, neighboring African nations, and throughout the world. To fully grasp the ups and downs that this coastal country has endured, one has to begin before the French arrived, when the first indigenous cultures had access and rights to their own land. From there, Côte d'Ivoire was ruled by outsiders for many decades. Today, it reflects its diverse background, everywhere from architecture and food to language and art. History has left an indelible mark on Côte d'Ivoire, for better and for worse.

"We want to move forward, certainly, but without denying our past." —Félix Houphouët-Boigny, first president of Côte d'Ivoire

CLANS

Independent clan kingdoms flourished in Côte d'Ivoire for many centuries before Europeans became interested in exploring the African continent. Unfortunately, very little is known about these kingdoms prior to the arrival of European ships in the 1460s, although it is thought that a Neolithic culture had existed. What is clear, however, is that from as early as the eighth century CE, Côte d'Ivoire was an important center for the many trade routes that fanned north across the Sahara Desert. Traders exchanged gold, kola nuts, and slaves for cloth, utensils, and salt.

Like many West African countries, Côte d'Ivoire was affected by the Atlantic slave trade.

THE SLAVE TRADE

The first sustained European interest in Africa developed in the late fifteenth century under the tutelage of the prince of Portugal. The Portuguese were motivated by a variety of impulses—a desire for knowledge, a wish to bring Christianity to the people, the search for potential allies against the Muslims, and the hope of finding slaves and lucrative new trade routes.

The Portuguese established a chain of trading settlements along the West African coast. African gold, ivory, foodstuffs, and slaves were exchanged for ironware, firearms, textiles, and European foods. The new trade had radical effects. Previous trade routes had been drawn across the Sahara. When they were redirected to the coast, battles soon flared up among the coastal people for control over trade and access to firearms from Europe. The situation attracted other Europeans who, throughout the sixteenth century, attempted to take over the existing trade.

Fortunately for the inhabitants of Côte d'Ivoire, European slaving and merchant ships preferred trafficking in other areas along the coast, such as Sierra Leone and Ghana, as they had better natural harbors.

European entrepreneurs were attracted to the region not only because of a promising ivory and gold trade but also because there was a seemingly endless supply of new people to enslave. From the sixteenth century to the nineteenth century, about 12.5 million people were kidnapped from their homes

Although France was the only country to settle in Côte d'Ivoire, many other countries, such as Portugal, had set foot in the country before France. Côte d'Ivoire has always maintained friendly relations with the West, particularly with France. Its relations with the United States have also been friendly and trustful. Côte d'Ivoire became a member of the United Nations (UN) in 1960 and has since benefited from its involvement. The UN sent peacekeepers to the country between 2004 and 2017 in order to help keep peace between the northern and southern regions. In June 2017, the UN officially closed its peacekeeping mission in Côte d'Ivoire.

in Africa. Over 10 million arrived in the Americas, where they were held in bondage. The transatlantic slave trade was a forced global migration that left the populations of African countries completely decimated. The slave trade was active not only in the United States but also in the Caribbean, Dutch Guiana, and Brazil. According to estimations, about 2 percent of those Africans who were enslaved were brought from present-day Côte d'Ivoire and Liberia.

In 1807, after years of profiting from slave trading, Great Britain moved to abolish it. Their decision led to increased Christian missionary activity in the region. Following on the heels of the missionaries were the European explorers, and their excursions stimulated the interest of merchants searching for new markets. However, the slave trade did not end with Great Britain's decision. It continued in other countries, through legal and illegal means, until the 1880s, when Brazil's smuggler ring ended after emancipation was granted there.

A FRENCH COLONY

France set up its first settlement in Côte d'Ivoire in 1637 when missionaries arrived in Assinie, near present-day Ghana. It wasn't until the early nineteenth century, though, that French merchants and their government became interested in Côte d'Ivoire, and they wholeheartedly began to exploit opportunities in the country. With gifts and cash, the French government enticed local chiefs in the 1840s to grant French commercial traders a monopoly along the coast in exchange for annual rents and French protection.

The French then built naval bases to keep out other traders. After signing treaties with the coastal chiefs, they moved inland to begin a systematic conquest of the interior. There they met fierce guerrilla resistance from the indigenous peoples and became embroiled in a long war.

Côte d'Ivoire became a French colony in 1893 and part of French West Africa by 1904. French imposition of forced labor and head taxes provoked passionate resistance, especially among the Baule, Anyi, and Abe (Abbey) peoples. New revolts broke out when France conscripted, or enlisted, thousands of Ivorians to serve with other West African soldiers in World War I. Such defiance continued until 1918, causing the French to become increasingly authoritarian in their efforts to hang on to power.

The French had one goal—to stimulate the production of exports. They planted coffee, cacao, and oil palms along the coast, and changed existing patterns of trade and of political, economic, and religious practices. They built transportation systems so that raw materials could be hauled easily to ports for export. Heavy-handed tax policies were instituted, forcing subsistence farmers to increase their production of cash crops or be swept into migrant labor.

In other parts of Africa, the French and English were largely colonial bureaucrats who would eventually return to their home countries. Côte d'Ivoire was the only West African country with a sizable population of foreign settlers. As a result, a third of the cacao, coffee, and banana plantations were in the hands of French citizens. The forced labor system, greatly hated by the Africans, became the backbone of the economy. At the time of independence, Côte d'Ivoire was French West Africa's most prosperous country, accounting for over 40 percent of the region's total exports.

A FIGHT FOR FREEDOM

After World War I, concerted efforts toward economic development were made. The French paid greater attention to providing education, health services, and development assistance, and to safeguarding local land rights. However, it was already too late. During the World War II years, a nationalist movement began to emerge, and the wish for independence grew. In 1944, a Baule chief named Félix Houphouët-Boigny founded a union of Ivorian farmers, the African Agricultural Union. This organization had several objectives—to secure better prices for African products, to eliminate practices that benefited only European farm owners, and to abolish forced labor.

Palm oil is an important export in Côte d'Ivoire. Here, people are moving seed pods onto a truck at a palm oil plantation.

From this organization emerged the first major African political party, the Democratic Party of Côte d'Ivoire (PDCI), led by Houphouët-Boigny. The PDCI met with opposition from the French administration because such a nationalistic party threatened French control. Tensions escalated into violence in 1949. Fortunately, Houphouët-Boigny had a remarkable ability to reconcile opponents, and this sustained the country's peaceful and prosperous relations with its West African neighbors and with France throughout most of his rule. In light of escalating tensions, he reversed his nationalistic policy and began to cooperate with the French.

On December 4, 1958, Côte d'Ivoire was proclaimed a republic by the French. After the national elections in 1959, Houphouët-Boigny emerged as premier. In 1960, after the French granted independence, he was elected president. Houphouët-Boigny remained president of Côte d'Ivoire until his death in 1993. Indeed, the nation's contemporary political history is, in fact, closely associated with his career.

POST-INDEPENDENCE

After Houphouët-Boigny became the country's first president, his government gave farmers good prices for their cash crops in order to stimulate production. The focus of development was on methods to improve farming. Coffee production increased significantly, and though it has fallen in export value, it remains a favorite crop and business venture for many families in the southeast. Coffee enjoys a privileged position in the French market because of low production costs and high demand. Cocoa production achieved similar results. Cacao beans became the main export, and their cultivation engages more than one-quarter of the population. By 1979, the country had become the world's leading cocoa producer, overtaking Ghana. It also became Africa's leading exporter of pineapples and palm oil. This "Ivorian miracle" was created with the help of French bureaucrats.

In the rest of Africa, Europeans were driven out by the liberated peoples following independence, but in Côte d'Ivoire the foreigners poured in, a result of Houphouët-Boigny's efforts to secure grants of French aid and attract a large number of French business interests. The French community ballooned from ten thousand to fifty thousand. Most of these newcomers were teachers and advisers.

After independence, Côte d'Ivoire was ruled by a one-party regime. Houphouët-Boigny's Democratic Party was the only legal party, and all members of the executive and legislative branches pledged allegiance to it. A free press did not exist—the only newspapers were government-owned. Opposition parties were outlawed, and freedom of expression, whether spoken or written, was prohibited.

As long as the economy prospered, Ivorians did not complain loudly about the lack of liberties. For twenty years, throughout the 1960s and 1970s, the economy maintained an annual growth rate of 10 percent. There were occasional protests against the president's conservatism, but they never merited military intervention. In 1973, for instance, a conspiracy by army officers was thwarted; in 1980, an attempt on the president's life was made; and in early 1983, student unrest caused the temporary shutdown of the university in Abidjan.

CONFLICT

Political upheaval and strained foreign relations became increasingly evident from the late 1980s. In 1986, the economy worsened. Coffee and cocoa prices dropped, and a world recession followed. Citizens voiced their displeasure with the government, demanded greater respect for human rights, and renewed their interest in a multiparty parliamentary democracy.

Both the external debt and crime in Abidjan increased threefold. The government took measures to restore economic growth, but these makeshift actions were not welcomed by the general public because they failed to improve the standard of living for most people. At the peak of the economic crisis, President Houphouët-Boigny was forced to call in the International Monetary Fund (IMF) for help with debt payment. Hundreds of civil servants went on strike, and students joined in violent street protests, resulting in five student deaths. The unrest was unparalleled in its scale and vigor. An investigating committee concluded that the military was responsible for the deaths, but the government refused to take action. As a result, people began rioting. After months of instability, Houphouët-Boigny was forced to legitimize other political parties, and Côte d'Ivoire's first multiparty elections were held in 1990. Independent newspapers were also allowed to begin publishing divergent views.

In this photo from 1967, President Felix Houphouët-Boigny signs papers at his desk.

Although the 1990 elections were opened to other political parties for the first time, Houphouët-Boigny succeeded in defeating challenger Laurent Gbagbo of the Ivorian Popular Front (FPI) and was elected to his seventh term. He received 85 percent of the vote, however, instead of his usual 99.9 percent. Houphouët-Boigny died in office in 1993, at the age of eighty-eight, and was peacefully replaced by his handpicked successor, the speaker of the National Assembly, Henri Konan Bédié. Bédié later won the election of 1995, one that was boycotted by most of the opposition.

Unlike Houphouët-Boigny—who was very careful to avoid ethnic conflict, leaving access to administrative posts open to immigrants from neighboring countries—Bédié emphasized the concept of "Ivority." Under Bédié, the government attempted to rewrite the constitution in a bid to prevent certain challengers who were not of "pure" Ivorian descent from running in presidential elections. This led to ethnic and religious tensions that escalated during his rule. On December 23, 1999, soldiers mutinied, ending three decades of religious and ethnic harmony forged by Houphouët-Boigny and toppling Bédié. Bédié fled, but not before planting seeds of ethnic discord by trying to stir up xenophobia against Muslim northerners, including his main rival, Alassane Ouattara.

Brigadier General Robert Gueï, a former member of Houphouët-Boigny's government, took control of the country the following day. Although Gueï announced that he would allow legislative and presidential elections by October 2000 in which he would not be a candidate, he changed his mind and ran for president. He also adopted and promoted the theme of xenophobia, banning Ouattara from the election because of his alleged foreign parentage. The 2000 election was a controversial one that saw Gueï attempt to manipulate the outcome. Gueï proclaimed himself president, but he was eventually deposed in a popular uprising that year, and he was replaced by Laurent Gbagbo.

After the 1999 military coup that had opened the door for General Gueï, there were hopes for recovery with a National Reconciliation Forum held in 2001. These hopes were shattered following a failed coup in 2002, in which Gueï was killed.

THE FIRST CIVIL WAR

The failed coup fueled unrest and ignited a civil war, voicing the ongoing discontent of northern Muslims who felt that they were being discriminated against in Ivorian politics. The brief onset of hostilities led to a severe deterioration in socioeconomic and humanitarian conditions. About seven hundred thousand people were displaced, and many thousands were killed. The country was pulled apart, with the government retaining control of the south and central regions, and the rebels—called the New Forces—holding on to the north and west areas. Peacekeeping troops from France, the Economic Community of West African States (ECOWAS), and eventually from the United Nations created a buffer zone between the rebels and the government troops.

After months of conflict, a peace agreement was concluded in 2003, but the cultural and nationalistic issues that caused the civil war, such as land ownership, the basis of nationality, and qualifications for holding office, were never entirely resolved. Despite a Security Council resolution mandating a UN peacekeeping mission with forces supported by the French military, simmering tensions exploded in 2004 when the government violated the cease-fire agreement by bombing rebel-held areas in the north.

In 2005, peace talks held in South Africa led to a new cease-fire agreement between the Ivorian government and the rebels. Both sides agreed to end the war. The terms of the agreement were not immediately implemented, however, and once again the fighting flared up.

Gbagbo's original term as president expired in 2005, but because of a lack of disarmament and the continuation of violence, it was nearly impossible to hold an election. On the basis of a plan worked out by the African Union and endorsed by the UN Security Council, Gbagbo's term was extended for another year. Even though the rebels rejected the possibility of yet another term extension for Gbagbo in 2006, the extension was endorsed by the United Nations once again under its plan to find lasting peace.

TEMPORARY PEACE

In 2007, following talks in Burkina Faso, President Laurent Gbagbo and New Forces leader Guillaume Soro announced that they had settled on a peace agreement aimed at reunifying the country and holding new elections in 2008. The Ouagadougou Political Agreement (OPA) was forged, and it foresaw the inauguration of a new transitional government. Soro was named prime minister. The transitional government announced that the buffer zone would be dismantled and the military would disarm. However, change did not come as easily or as smoothly as people hoped. Though rebels and soldiers did begin to withdraw from the buffer zone, violence continued. In June 2007, at an airport in the northern region, Prime Minister Soro's airplane came under violent attack, and four were killed in the gunfire. Throughout 2007 and 2008, the United Nations renewed the mandate for peacekeepers to stay in the nation and extended sanctions that had been imposed on the country. With the conflict ongoing, global assistance was needed, especially as presidential elections were delayed time and time again into 2010.

ELECTION AND AFTERMATH

Finally, in 2010, the first and second rounds of the presidential election were held. Alassane Ouattara was announced as the winner of a runoff election, with

Armed soldiers raise their weapons before the Battle of Abidjan in April 2011.

54 percent of the vote. However, the Constitutional Council and Gbagbo refused to accept defeat, declaring the election illegal and sealing the country's borders. Gbagbo was sworn in as president despite objections from the international community, telling the United Nations to leave Côte d'Ivoire. All the while, violent protests occurred in Abidjan and Yamoussoukro.

Over the next year, Gbagbo continued to retain a strong, forced grip on power within the country. The UN, neighboring countries, and Ouattara himself all attempted peace talks and tried to convince Gbagbo to resign. However, nothing worked, and the rebel forces took up arms again under a new name, the Republican Forces of the Ivory Coast, or FRCI. The new country-wide military offensive seized Abidjan, burned villages, and allegedly killed hundreds of civilians. In March 2011, a violent period of two days would be known as the Duékoué Massacre. Fighters with the pro-Ouattara militia groups took hold of the city of Duékoué on March 29, killing as many as eight hundred people. Violence and murders were reported on both sides of the conflict.

In April 2011, Gbagbo was captured from his bunker in Abidjan, and Ouattara was formally inaugurated as president. In the months that followed, ex-ministers who served under Gbagbo were charged with embezzlement and crimes against the state, and Gbagbo was taken into custody by the International Criminal Court in The Hague.

President Ouattara remains in power today, though his presidency has not been without conflict too. He has worked to bring stability to a country marked by armed attacks that are allegedly being carried out by supporters of Gbagbo from Ghana, the country's neighbor. In September 2012, the border between the two countries was closed. Additionally, President Ouattara temporarily dissolved the federal government in 2012 over a dispute involving marriage laws. Ouattara desired to make wives joint heads of household with their husbands, while members of Parliament wanted to keep the old laws, which recognized only men as decision-makers and heads of household.

RECENT EVENTS

Most recently, Côte d'Ivoire has been struggling against Islamist militants who have launched multiple assaults in the neighboring countries of Mali and Burkina Faso. In March 2016, militants attacked a beach resort at Grand-Bassam, killing nineteen people. Additionally, President Ouattara has been involved in stand-offs with the military and government workers, who have engaged in sporadic mutinies over nonpayment, poor working conditions, and other complaints.

A deadly attack in March 2016 targeted the resort town of Grand-Bassam. Here, a medical attendant carries an injured boy.

While the country is currently in a period of relative peace, time will tell if President Ouattara and Parliament, which is controlled by a majority made up of his allies, will be able to maintain strong, peaceful control over Côte d'Ivoire and move on from past violent conflicts. The process remains a fragile yet necessary step in the journey toward a united Côte d'Ivoire.

INTERNET LINKS

https://www.bbc.com/news/world-africa-13287585
This BBC timeline covers major events in Côte d'Ivoire's history.

https://www.britannica.com/place/Cote-dIvoire
This encyclopedic article gives an overview of the country, as well as information about its history.

https://www.state.gov/r/pa/ei/bgn/2846.htm
This federal fact sheet gives an overview of the relationship between the United States and Côte d'Ivoire.

GOVERNMENT

This photo shows newly elected senators who were inaugurated on April 5, 2018, in Yamoussoukro.

3

FOR MANY DECADES, THE RESIDENTS of Côte d'Ivoire were not in control of their government or its actions. As a colony, they possessed very little power. After independence, there have been numerous arguments—some of them violent—about how, exactly, the independent government should operate and who should be in charge. For nearly ten years, the government has been running relatively smoothly under its president. With a new constitution and the resulting second house of Parliament, Côte d'Ivoire can expect many changes resulting from the evolution of its structure. Increased transparency and new policies are likely outcomes. Time will tell how changes to the governmental structure will affect the day-to-day lives of Ivorians.

"I hear talk here and there that there are political tensions, it's not true. Ivory Coast wants to move forward."
—President Alassane Ouattara, July 2018

From independence to 1990, Côte d'Ivoire had a one-party government. All candidates for the National Assembly belonged to the PDCI, which was considered the only legal party. In 1990, however, other parties were legalized. Today, Côte d'Ivoire is a presidential republic. In the last presidential election, held in 2015, several political parties were represented, including the ruling Rally of Houphouëtists for Democracy and Peace (RHDP); Alliance of Democratic Forces; Renewal for Peace and Concord; and Liberty and Democracy for the Republic. Now, the country is gearing up for a 2020 election that some fear could turn violent. Ahead of the elections, President Ouattara is hoping to bring people together, keep them calm, and inspire optimism.

DECENTRALIZATION

Côte d'Ivoire is relatively decentralized, with many levels of control that fan out under the umbrella of the federal government. Reforms in 2011 provided for even further decentralization and reorganization. The country is divided into twelve districts and two autonomous regions, which are then divided further into thirty-one regions. Each region has a leader who is referred to as the "prefect." These regions are further divided into 108 departments, which have 510 sub-departments, called sub-prefectures. Departments can be thought of a bit like counties in the United States. They are usually named after the city or town that serves as the department's "seat." The departments are run by prefects who are appointed by the cabinet of the national government. Throughout the years, these administrative subdivisions of Côte d'Ivoire have changed, and the map has been drawn and redrawn many times, not unlike the redistricting that occurs within US states and Canadian provinces.

POLITICAL STRUCTURE

The political structure in Côte d'Ivoire has undergone change since the 1960s. Today, the country has executive, judicial, and legislative branches.

EXECUTIVE POWER is personified in the president, who is elected for a five-year term. Beginning with the 2020 election, the president will have a

Alassane Dramane Ouattara was a New Year's baby, born on January 1, 1942. He was born in the town of Dimbokro. His family was Muslim and part of the Dyula community, though opponents have long claimed that one or both of his parents hailed from nearby Burkina Faso. As a child, Ouattara received schooling in Côte d'Ivoire and Burkina Faso, then continued on to Drexel University in Philadelphia, Pennsylvania, where he earned a bachelor's degree in business administration. In 1967, he received a master's degree in economics, followed by a PhD in the same subject in 1972. He received both degrees at the University of Pennsylvania.

While completing his education, Ouattara took a job as an economist at the International Monetary Fund. In 1973, he left the IMF to head home, where he was employed at the Central Bank of West African States. In 1984, he went back to the IMF to head the African department.

It wasn't until the spring of 1990, when he was approaching his fiftieth birthday, that Ouattara entered the political arena. During a time of economic crisis, Ouattara was appointed to chair a special commission on economic recovery by then-president Houphouët-Boigny. Soon after, he was put into the newly created post of prime minister. Though his austerity measures were unpopular, Ouattara worked hard to bring the country back to a stable economic state.

Ouattara took over much of the work of the presidency as Houphouët-Boigny's health began to fail, and many hoped that he would assume the presidency. However, on the day of the president's death in 1993, Henri Konan Bédié, the president of the National Assembly and Houphouët-Boigny's preferred successor, quickly took over the office. A discouraged Ouattara left for the IMF once more, where he worked until 1999. During that time, he became the president of the Rally of Republicans, a political party within Côte d'Ivoire. He attempted to run for president of Côte d'Ivoire, but he was barred due to restrictions concerning parental birth and a candidate's continuous residency within the country. Though he was cleared to run in 2005, civil war sent the country into chaos, and Ouattara left to avoid threats of violence.

In 2010, Ouattara won the presidential election amid opposition from the outgoing president, who refused to back down, sparking protests, violence, and unrest across the country. All told, the violence would result in over three thousand deaths. Ouattara's rebel forces eventually defeated Gbagbo and his supporters, and Ouattara was installed as the official president. He remains in power today.

limit of two terms. This new rule was established by the 2016 constitution. The president of Côte d'Ivoire is the head of state and commander in chief of the armed forces. The president appoints a prime minister as head of his government. The prime minister, in turn, appoints a ministerial cabinet to carry out the work of the government. The new 2016 constitution also established the position of a vice president, who will be directly elected by the people beginning in 2020. In January 2017, President Alassane Ouattara appointed Daniel Kablan Duncan to be the country's first vice president. He is the second in command.

President Alassane Dramane Ouattara was first elected on December 4, 2010. However, at the time of his election, former president Gbagbo remained in power, refusing to step down until he was removed in 2011. Ouattara was reelected during the 2015 presidential election with 83 percent of the vote.

JUDICIAL POWER is based on French civil law, with the highest level of authority in the hands of the Supreme Court. A high court of justice has the authority to try government officials, even the president. Lower courts include the appellate, or court of appeals, state security, and court of first instance (an initial trial court).

As the country has become more modernized and begun to grow economically following times of political and civil unrest, the court systems have evolved to meet new needs. In rural areas, there are still some traditional village groups in place that handle domestic disputes and other local matters. However, each year, these forms of organized, local justice systems are being replaced by the formal court system. There are also formal military courts that try only members of the military, and in 2012, a Commercial Chamber of the Court of Appeals was established in order to handle a backlog of commercial cases. It is located in Abidjan. These reforms helped Côte d'Ivoire move up seventeen places on the World Bank's "ease of doing business" index in 2017.

LEGISLATIVE POWER is exercised by a bicameral, or two-house, Parliament. The National Assembly has 255 seats, with members directly elected in their constituencies. They serve five-year terms. The last National Assembly election was held on December 18, 2016. The next one will be held in 2021. The current president of the National Assembly is Guillaume Soro, who has served in that role since 2012. As of 2018, there are twenty-seven women in the National Assembly, making up about 10 percent of the group.

The Parliament also has a Senate. Its first-ever election was held on March 25, 2018. The Senate has ninety-nine seats. Sixty-six members are elected in each of the regions and districts by an electoral college system. Mayors, councilors, and members of the National Assembly make up the electoral college. The other thirty-three members of the Senate are appointed by the president. The president of the Senate is Jeannot Ahoussou-Kouadio. He was elected in 2018. There are eight elected female members of the Senate, making up 12 percent of the elected portion of the body.

At this time, both the Senate and National Assembly are dominated by the ruling party, RHDP.

In 2018, the newly inaugurated senators sported matching scarves in the colors of Côte d'Ivoire's flag.

NEW CONSTITUTION

On November 8, 2016, President Alassane Ouattara officially instituted the brand-new Ivorian constitution. About 93 percent of those who voted supported the new constitution, though those numbers were rejected by people in opposition, who insisted that the participation rate was grossly inflated and that the vote was marred by fraud.

Regardless, the new constitution established a new executive position, that of vice president. It is a position with a five-year term, just like the president. The constitution also established a bicameral Parliament, creating the Senate to serve alongside the National Assembly. While two-thirds of Senate members are elected by vote, thirty-three are appointed by the president. Additionally, the constitution removed an upper age limit of seventy-five for a presidential candidate and changed an older provision that mandated a presidential candidate must have two natural-born Ivorian parents. Today, a candidate need only have one natural-born Ivorian parent. Some posit that this old rule

A woman casts her vote in 2018. The government is working to rebuild citizens' trust in the electoral system.

was meant to exclude northern Ivorians, many of whom had parents from bordering countries, and even the current president himself was once banned from running due to the rule. He denied the allegations that his parents were from Burkina Faso.

ELECTION ISSUES

While independence provided much positive change for Côte d'Ivoire, it also produced many new issues, among them the question of elections. Over the last few decades, Ivorians have grown to deeply mistrust both their electoral systems and political parties. This culminated in the 2010 post-election violence that left nearly one million Ivorians displaced from their homes and at least three thousand dead. Elections, though they were relatively peaceful in 2015, are still in need of reforms, and many Ivorians fear that violence will erupt again following the 2020 elections. Violence and conflict arise when citizens do not trust their systems. Côte d'Ivoire has yet to rebuild total trust between its citizens and government, but it is working toward that goal. The International Foundation for Electoral Systems maintained a presence in the country between 2006 and 2017, working to strengthen citizens' knowledge, participation, and trust in the system. It helped build capacity, held roundtable discussions to facilitate dialogue, and distributed informational materials to polling places.

A HISTORY OF DISTRUST

Though policy changes and new personalities have emerged in Côte d'Ivoire, the country has a past riddled with political unrest, distrust, and even violence. In October 1995, major opposition parties boycotted the presidential election, citing irregularities in the electoral code and voter registration. They claimed that the government used the 1994 electoral code to place formidable obstacles in the path of political rivals. One of the opposition parties, the Rally of Republicans (RDR), held that Alassane Ouattara, a leading rival to Henri Konan Bédié, had been unfairly excluded from entering the presidential race.

The opposition also complained that there were not enough checks to ensure that prospective voters were eligible. They denounced restrictions on marches and sit-ins three months prior to the election, which had been an attempt to guarantee public order. The opposition called for an active boycott of the presidential election. They blocked access to polling stations and prevented delivery of election materials. Talks between the government and opposition groups broke down over this issue, despite concessions on both sides. The dispute left at least five people dead.

In early November 1995, negotiations between the government and the opposition parties led to an agreement in which the controversial electoral lists would be revised. As a result, the boycott was lifted, and nine opposition parties challenged the ruling PDCI for the 175 parliamentary seats. A number of independent candidates, some of whom had left the PDCI, also joined the race.

Despite these negotiations and changes, a National Assembly election held in December 2000 once again plunged Côte d'Ivoire into chaos. It was marred by violence, irregularities, and a low participation rate of 33 percent. At least forty people were killed in Abidjan alone. The continued RDR boycott in protest of the invalidation of the candidacy of party president Alassane Ouattara was largely to blame for the low participation. In addition, the election could not be held in twenty-six electoral districts in the north because RDR activists had disrupted polling stations, burned ballots, and threatened the safety of election officials. In 2010, another chaotic election ended in violence between supporters of the incoming president, Ouattara, and supporters of the outgoing Gbagbo, who refused to give up his seat.

ARMED FORCES OF CÔTE D'IVOIRE

Since the outbreak of violence in September 2002 that split the country, as well as the 2010—2011 civil war, the nation's military has undergone multiple restructuring efforts. The former system that broke the country into four military regions no longer exists.

Today, the military is referred to as the Republican Forces of the Ivory Coast, or FRCI. This new national military has roots in the rebel coalition Forces Nouvelles de Côte d'Ivoire that was established in March 2011 to fight against

In 2017, Ivorian soldiers joined UN Peacekeepers in Mali for a peacekeeping mission. Here, the soldiers are marching.

the Ivorian army and outgoing President Gbagbo. With the help of the French military, the Forces Nouvelles de Côte d'Ivoire was able to overthrow Gbagbo and establish the FRCI. In recent years, the army has had difficulties when it comes to integrating Gbagbo supporters into the army. Additionally, wage disputes have resulted in mutinies, though the current ruling government ultimately settled financially with the FRCI, and it remains the national military.

Côte d'Ivoire has an army, air force, and navy. The army is the largest branch of the armed forces, with thousands of members, though active membership has changed over the years, especially during times of war. Currently, there is no set system of military regions, as there had been in years past. Instead, there are several active units and bases throughout the country, as well as special forces branches. Most of the Ivorian army's equipment was procured from France during the 1980s, though Gbagbo's presidency saw large quantities of second-hand Soviet weapons enter the country. Other armored cars, tanks, and vehicles have come from South Africa, Sweden, and the United States.

The Ivorian Air Force's function is to defend the nation's airspace. In addition, it provides transportation support to other services. In 2004, under orders from Gbagbo, the military forces engaged in air strikes on Ivorian rebels, attacking French peacekeepers in rebel-held towns. Multiple French soldiers were wounded and killed. Côte d'Ivoire maintained that the rebels were the targets, and that the French deaths were unintentional, while France disagreed. In response, France acted quickly, moving into the Yamoussoukro airport and destroying the entirety of the air force's helicopters and airplanes. Since then, the air force has been in a state of rebuilding. As of 2018, the air force has two presidential jets, four helicopters, and a jet trainer.

Côte d'Ivoire maintains a brown-water navy for coastal surveillance and security for the nation's 320-mile (515 km) coastline. The operational capability of the navy's vessels has degraded since the nation's two civil wars, and the navy is unable to carry out its missions beyond the general area of Abidjan.

In 1961, France and Côte d'Ivoire signed a mutual defense accord providing for the stationing of French forces in Côte d'Ivoire. Shortly after the start of the hostilities in 2002, France deployed troops primarily to protect French nationals, but this move also aided Ivorian forces. In January 2003, an economic union known as the Economic Community of West African States (ECOWAS) also placed about 1,500 peacekeeping troops from five countries. These troops later became part of the UN Operation in Côte d'Ivoire (UNOCI). After the signing of the Ouagadougou Political Agreement (OPA) in 2007, the number of such troops fell steadily in light of the progress the Ivorians made. The UN Security Council continued to extend the UNOCI's mandate until it officially ended in 2017.

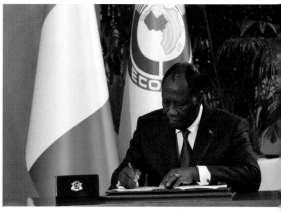

On November 8, 2016, President Alassane Ouattara signed the new Ivorian constitution.

FREEDOMS

Although the constitution provides for freedom of expression, in reality this liberty is still restricted. The government does not tolerate what it considers insults or attacks on the honor or dignity of the country's highest officials, and such offenses are punishable by prison sentences. Insulting the president is a crime, and the government keeps a close watch on the media sector as a whole. In fact, the Paris-based media watchdog Reporters Without Borders ranks the country eighty-second on its list of 180 countries in terms of press freedom. In 2017, eight journalists were taken into custody, but the National Assembly also adopted a law in December 2017 that states that there are no admissible grounds for detaining journalists. A 2004 law decriminalized most media offenses. The constitution also protects freedom of assembly but requires opposition parties to request permits before holding public rallies. If rallies are held without proper permits, organizers can be tried and convicted.

Despite these concerns, the media environment has generally become less restrictive in recent years. State-run media outlets continue to dominate everything from radio to television, but independent operations are expanding,

The army is the largest branch of the armed forces. Paramilitary forces include a presidential guard and the gendarmerie (the national police force).

and the media has been largely free to cover the most recent elections. There is no official censorship, and most fears have dissipated since the new president took office. In 2016, four new private television stations were awarded licenses, and most press-related offenses have been decriminalized.

HUMAN RIGHTS

In May 2017, mutinous soldiers gathered in the cities to demand bonus payments.

The government has cooperated with international inquiries into its human rights practices, but various human rights organizations have alleged that although there has been some improvement, particularly after the signing of the 2007 Ouagadougou Agreement, abuses persist. The United Nations ended a thirteen-year peacekeeping mission in the country in 2017, but violent army mutinies have marred the country's peace in recent months. In its 2018 report, the Human Rights Watch, a global nongovernmental organization, expressed concerns about causes of past conflicts that remain unaddressed, such as the politicized judiciary system and continued conflicts over land. When it comes to the judiciary, arbitrary arrests and mistreatment of prisoners are down overall, but there are still few investigations into those who commit abuses.

Additionally, the mutinies and demonstrations by soldiers demanding unpaid bonuses have resulted in protests, injuries, and deaths. In May 2017, mutinying soldiers found an arms cache, which aided in their ability to extort the government. The UN says that the nation has failed to complete the disarmament process and to properly secure weapons, putting the country in danger of future mutinies and protests.

According to a 2017 UN report, cases of gender-based violence have decreased since 2014, though many victims do not report abuses for fear of social stigma. The new constitution does not protect against discrimination on

CHILD SOLDIER PREVENTION ACT

In 2007, the US Congress introduced the Child Soldier Prevention Act that is crafted to encourage governments around the world to disarm, demobilize, and rehabilitate child soldiers from government forces and government-supported militias. UNICEF estimates that about five thousand child soldiers took part in the successive civil wars in Côte d'Ivoire. Currently, the nation is experiencing a time of relative peace, but in 2012, supporters of former president Gbagbo began recruiting child soldiers in Liberia to commit attacks on the western edge of Côte d'Ivoire.

the grounds of sexual orientation, and incidents, including physical assaults, against LGBTQ persons are common.

Human trafficking—including children for forced labor, prostitution, and armed assault—is also a problem in Côte d'Ivoire. While the government does not currently meet the standards for elimination of trafficking in its country, it is making efforts to do so. In both 2010 and 2016, the government passed new laws that would further help find, convict, and sentence those involved in human trafficking.

The legal code in Côte d'Ivoire does not define domestic violence, which is a serious problem in the country. Female victims of domestic violence suffer severe social stigmatization and, as a result, often will not report or discuss domestic violence. Women's advocacy groups continue to protest the indifference of authorities to such crimes. These groups, such as the Association of Women Lawyers and the National Council for Women, created with help from the UN, also continue to sponsor campaigns against the ongoing issues of forced marriages, marriage of minors, and practices that are considered harmful to women and girls. Even though the law prohibits forced marriages, they still take place throughout the country. Unfortunately, tribal marriages are commonly performed with girls as young as fourteen.

Other human rights issues that currently impact the country include overcrowded prisons, violent crimes enacted by street gangs, and public lynching of suspected criminals. The nation's Special Investigative and Examination Cell has launched investigations into human rights crimes committed during the

2010—2011 civil war. While many perpetrators have been charged from both sides, including pro-Ouattara commanders, the fairness of some trials has been questioned, notably the trial of former first lady Simone Gbagbo. At the end of 2011, President Ouattara set up the Dialogue, Truth, and Reconciliation Commission, an institution that was tasked with promoting reconciliation and renewing cohesion among Ivorians. In 2014, the final report of the commission was published, giving recommendations for implementation. Meanwhile, the country's reparations group was disbanded in 2017 after awarding cash payments, medical care, and nonmonetary assistance to victims of the 2010 civil war. The governmental group identified over three hundred thousand victims. As of 2018, the International Criminal Court (ICC) trial of Laurent Gbagbo is ongoing. Gbagbo is being held in the Netherlands as he awaits the end of his trial, which began in 2016.

GLOBAL REACH

There is no doubt that Côte d'Ivoire has played an important and constructive role in the region and has maintained close ties with its African counterparts. Looking beyond the African continent, Côte d'Ivoire also has a foreign policy that is favorable to the West, and it has been a member of the United Nations since independence in 1960.

Even though Côte d'Ivoire's foreign policy maintains a variety of diplomatic contacts, France has always been the nation's single most important foreign partner. Félix Houphouët-Boigny was a minister in the French government before Côte d'Ivoire's independence, and he insisted that the country's relationship with France remain strong after he became president. Gallic influences are seen everywhere in Côte d'Ivoire, and many of the country's internal systems are modeled after the French.

Côte d'Ivoire also maintains a sound relationship with the United States. The United States has assisted in global efforts to help the country move past its decades of crisis. It works to encourage continued disarmament, restore peace, and help reunify the country. Additionally, it focuses assistance on advancing reform in the security sector, providing economic opportunity, improving health-care systems, and strengthening democracy. It does this through capacity-building, technical assistance, and expansion of access to treatment and prevention for HIV/AIDS as well as malaria. In 2017, the United States and Côte d'Ivoire signed a $524.7 million Millennium Challenge Corporation contract to facilitate bilateral trade and improve vocational education.

Apart from financial aid, the United States and Côte d'Ivoire conduct several active cultural exchange programs, which enables Ivorian students, scholars, government officials, civic leaders, media representatives, and educators to visit the United States, better acquainting them with the American people. These programs also send US citizens to Côte d'Ivoire. These visits facilitate an exchange of ideas and views.

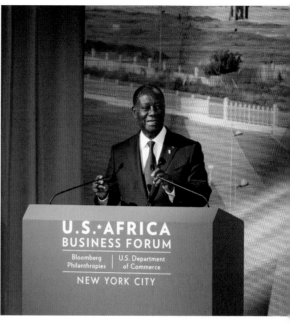

President Ouattara participates in the US-Africa Business Forum held in New York City in 2016.

INTERNET LINKS

https://www.cia.gov/library/publications/the-world-factbook/geos/iv.html

This is the CIA World Factbook page for Côte d'Ivoire.

http://country.eiu.com/article.aspx?articleid=444530628&Country=C%C3%B4te%20d%27Ivoire&topic=Summary&subtopic=Political+structure

The *Economist* offers a breakdown of Côte d'Ivoire's political structure.

https://onuci.unmissions.org/en

Here, you can read all about the United Nations' peacekeeping operation in Côte d'Ivoire, which ended in 2017.

ECONOMY

Paper CFA francs are brightly colored and patterned.

4

The 2018 Index of Economic Freedom gave Côte d'Ivoire an overall score of 62.0, ranking it eighty-fifth in the world for economic freedom.

THOUGH THE STATE OF THE government system or military can tell us a lot about a country, the economy is another important indicator. A healthy economy can be a sign of wise decisions made in the past, day-to-day stability, and even hope for the future. There are no economies that are 100 percent stable or prosperous at all times. As with other developing countries, the economy of Côte d'Ivoire has gone through multiple evolutions, stark changes, and seemingly small steps that build toward greater health and strength. By reviewing its past and current conditions, we can learn much about what the future might hold for this West African nation.

AGRICULTURAL RELIANCE

The economy of Côte d'Ivoire relies primarily on agriculture. It had a good financial reputation for many years but has also experienced significant

Today, gold mines like this one are big business in Côte d'Ivoire.

drops and changes in the world prices of cocoa and coffee—Côte d'Ivoire's two leading agricultural exports. Political instability since the late 1990s took a heavy toll on economic growth, disrupted trade, and widened poverty. However, the country's current economy is headed in the right direction.

With the election of President Ouattara, Côte d'Ivoire has been on the road to economic health. In fact, over the last five years, the country's economic growth rate has been among the highest in the world. It continues to be one of the largest producers and exporters of coffee, cocoa beans, and palm oil, the prices of which all fluctuate according to changes in the climate and the global economy. Growing industries outside of agriculture include gold mining and the exporting of electricity.

DEBT AND AID

Many African countries do not have readily available funds to develop their economies in meaningful, lasting ways, and foreign private enterprises have often considered investment in these underdeveloped areas too risky. Thus, the major alternative sources of financing are national and multinational lending institutions, such as the World Bank and the IMF. In 2008, the World Bank announced that Côte d'Ivoire had fully paid its arrears, paving the way for new assistance. In the following year, the IMF agreed to lend Côte d'Ivoire $565 million. Attached to the loan were strict conditions relating to poverty reduction and financial transparency that Côte d'Ivoire had to adhere to.

Côte d'Ivoire's national debt stood at $13.07 billion in 2017, having grown steadily since 2012's relative low of $9.5 billion. With economist President Ouattara at the helm, the country is working toward a goal of becoming an emerging market by 2020. Over the past five years, determined political reforms, paired with economic growth, have attracted both investment and development funds, and the GDP has seen an increase of 9 percent over each of the last five years. Public sector spending on infrastructure and other government

Côte d'Ivoire's gold mining industry continues to grow with help from the government. In January 2018, the Ivorian federal government awarded gold prospecting licenses to three companies searching for gold ore deposits across the eastern, northern, and southwestern regions of the country. In recent years, production in the country has been booming, doubling between 2013 and 2015. The country sits on vast deposits of gold ore in the Birimian Greenstone Belt, an area full of ancient rocks that often contain large deposits of valuable minerals. Gold mines in Côte d'Ivoire can employ thousands of workers and produce many tons of gold each year. The Ivorian "gold rush" doesn't seem to be stopping anytime soon.

investments have driven much of the economic expansion, but the country will need to attract even more participation from the private sector if it wants to continue to grow.

In 2017, Côte d'Ivoire signed a five-year, $524.7 million compact with the Millennium Challenge Corporation, an aid agency operated by the US government. The grant seeks to spur economic growth and reduce poverty, especially by supporting new businesses and supporting stability. Côte d'Ivoire is expected to contribute $22 million to the budget on its own. Projects specific to the MCC grant include the Skills for Employability and Productivity Project. This project aims to increase access to secondary education through construction of up to eighty-four new schools. It also seeks to overcome gender disparities and help girls succeed in school. Meanwhile, the Abidjan Transport Project will focus on road rehabilitation and improving road network management.

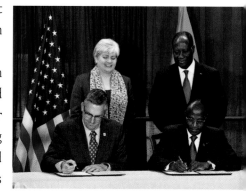

Representatives from the Millennium Challenge Corporation and Côte d'Ivoire jointly sign a new agreement in 2017.

EXPORTS

The economy is largely market-based, and it depends heavily on the agricultural sector. About two-thirds of the people living in Côte d'Ivoire are engaged in some aspect of agricultural activities. Reliance on commodity exports, however,

Established in 2004 by the George W. Bush administration, the Millennium Challenge Corporation (MCC) is a US foreign aid agency. Its focus is to promote economic growth in the countries that receive its support, and it seeks to be free from political influence. Authorized with bipartisan support, the MCC is guided by principles of competitive selection of countries, country-led priorities, and country-led implementation. Today, it has an annual budget of about $800 million and employs three hundred people in its Washington, DC, offices. Over the years, the MCC has invested over $12 billion in worldwide programs that support projects aimed at tackling issues related to health, land rights, transportation, water supply, education, sanitation, agriculture, and so much more.

In December 2018, Côte d'Ivoire was found eligible for concurrent compacts, opening up the possibility for a second partnership between the MCC and Côte d'Ivoire, this time incorporating four other countries in West Africa: Benin, Burkina Faso, Ghana, and Niger. The MCC hopes that these larger, regional investments will spur economic growth within the area as a whole.

exposes the economy to the ups and downs of international price swings as well as to changes in weather.

To end the country's dependence on fluctuating world prices for cocoa and coffee, the government encourages export diversification and intermediate processing of cacao beans. As a result, a light industrial sector has arisen, producing textiles, chemicals, and sugar for export. A few assembly plants for cars and other manufactured goods also have been built and are making significant headway. The country has also worked hard to expand exports of electricity and gold.

COCOA AND COFFEE

Côte d'Ivoire is the world's largest producer and exporter of cocoa. A large amount of the population is engaged in the production of cocoa. The country is also a leading producer of coffee. These two commodities make up half of the country's export earnings. Besides cocoa and coffee, the government encourages the production of cotton, bananas, rubber, rice, palm kernels, sweet potatoes, sugar, and cassava. Cassava, more commonly known as tapioca, is widely grown because it does well in eroded soils. Along the coast, coconut trees and pineapples are also grown.

Despite such massive domestic production, Côte d'Ivoire imports much of the food eaten by its citizens, such as rice, dairy products, corn, wheat, and meat. This disparity is because planted land is used primarily for commercial cash crops, and local people farm on a subsistence basis. Goats and sheep are the most significant livestock raised, since cows cannot be kept in areas infested with tsetse flies.

In May 2018, the World Bank approved a credit of $70 million from the International Development Association that will help rural communities in Côte d'Ivoire receive more access to digital services, which can then be used to improve farm productivity and gain access to markets. This will be important in the future, especially as climate change and expected temperature rises have an impact on plant growth. Reports from 2017 and even earlier suggest that temperature rises caused by climate change may leave many West African areas completely unable to grow cocoa. Researchers across the globe are looking into new cocoa varieties that can tolerate higher temperatures and resist diseases, which often plague the beans.

INDUSTRY

The larger manufacturing industries include food-processing plants, lumber and textile mills, car assembly plants, steel container and aluminum sheet production, and oil refineries. Although the economy is still heavily dependent on agriculture, oil and gas production since 2006 have become important engines of economic activity. Côte d'Ivoire's offshore oil and gas production have resulted in substantial crude oil exports. In 2017, oil production reached fifty-four thousand barrels per day. Côte d'Ivoire has a complex refinery at Abidjan.

Côte d'Ivoire's offshore oil and gas production provide sufficient natural gas to fuel electricity exports to Ghana, Togo, Benin, Mali, and Burkina Faso.

Côte d'Ivoire's timber industry produces wood for flooring, particle board, plywood, and more.

TIMBER

Côte d'Ivoire is a major exporter of hardwood. In the mid-1970s, timber overtook coffee to become the principal export. Since then, more sawmills and wood-processing plants have been built to produce plywood, crates, railroad ties, boxes, veneers, cabinets, and furniture. While timber is no longer the main export, it is still important to the country's economy. The major export markets for Côte d'Ivoire's hardwood products are Italy, Spain, Germany, France, the United Kingdom, India, Belgium, Romania, and the United States.

MINING THE EARTH

Known reserves of copper, nickel, uranium, and manganese exist far below the earth across Côte d'Ivoire. Foreign investment is driving a renewed interest in mining, especially gold mining, which is becoming a booming industry in Côte d'Ivoire. Diamonds used to be the "glimmering" export. About 12,000 carats of diamonds were unearthed each year. In 2005, however, the United Nations banned the export of diamonds from Côte d'Ivoire. This ban was imposed as part of an arms embargo designed to prevent northern rebels from acquiring weapons illicitly through the sale of diamonds. The ban was lifted in 2014, and the country set about rebuilding an industry that had leaned on illegal means for nearly a decade. The industry is still getting used to legally extracting and exporting diamonds again.

TOURISTS

With a long coastal strip of beautiful beaches and lagoons, as well as protected wildlife and a lavish cultural heritage, Côte d'Ivoire has plenty to attract tourists. Tourism has the potential of becoming a leading industry, but a great many more capital resources need to be poured into the building of hotels and tourist inducements. Multiple civil wars and recent terrorist attacks have slowed the stream of tourists into the country. In 2011, tourism accounted for just 0.6 percent of the country's GDP. In 2016, this percentage rose to 7.5 percent. This growth is an indicator that Ivorians may want to continue investing in their tourism industry, as it could offer even more economic opportunities in the coming years. The growth also matches a wider trend of growth in travel to Africa as a continent. International tourism, of which Europeans make up about half, continues to grow at a rate of about 6 percent per year.

FOREIGN TRADING

Foreign trading consists largely of imports of petroleum products, consumer goods, food, machinery, and transportation equipment, and exports of coffee, cocoa, palm oil, timber, petroleum, bananas, and pineapples. In 2017, annual exports totaled $11.74 billion, and imports amounted to $9.44 billion. Principal trading partners for exports are the Netherlands, the United States, France, Germany, Belgium, Burkina Faso, India, and Mali. Chief partners for imports are Nigeria, France, China, and the United States.

MONEY

Côte d'Ivoire is a member of the eight-nation West African Economic and Monetary Union. The currency is the African Financial Community (CFA) franc, with convertibility guaranteed by the French treasury. The West African CFA franc has been pegged to the euro at a rate of 663.61 CFA francs per euro. The West African CFA franc coins and banknotes are not accepted in countries using Central African CFA francs, and vice versa. In January 2019, one US dollar equaled 581 West African CFA francs on average.

TRANSPORTATION AND COMMUNICATION

Côte d'Ivoire has a very advanced infrastructure by the standards of developing countries. There is a network of paved roads, and telecommunications services include cellular phones, internet access, and a public data communications network. Ivorians have their choice of popular streaming services, including Netflix and Amazon. A startup video-on-demand company, Afrostream,

Here, electric three-wheeled taxis (red vehicles) travel throughout Jacqueville, a coastal city. They are seen in other cities as well.

> ## USE OF RENEWABLE ENERGY

As climate change continues to be a hot-button subject around the world, programs and investors are looking to countries like Côte d'Ivoire and investigating their potential for renewable energy development. Studies completed in 2018 suggest that Côte d'Ivoire houses enormous opportunities for renewable energy solutions. In Abidjan, some power is already being produced by a hydroelectric dam, and the city is planning a solar power station, as well as a biomass-based power plant.

The country is hoping to reduce its greenhouse gas emissions by 2030, in line with the commitments laid out by the Paris Climate Agreement. With many areas seeing plenty of sunshine per day, the country has the potential to harness solar energy in productive and profitable ways. Researchers estimate that there is potential for more hydropower plants, as well as biomass projects. There is no specific wind data available aside from wind speeds detected by airport professionals.

launched in 2015 but was unable to stay profitable and ultimately closed its doors in 2017. Iroko+ is a popular streaming service that features Nollywood films, or movies made by the Nigerian film industry.

There are multiple active ports. The port of Abidjan is the most modern in West Africa and the largest between Casablanca and Cape Town. Abidjan has a fully equipped international airport, located at Port-Bouët, as well as a few smaller airports. A smaller port operates in San-Pédro. In the fall of 2017, the Japan International Cooperation Agency issued a loan totaling over $100 million to Côte d'Ivoire for further investment in and development of its ports. The main airlines that fly in the country include Ethiopian Airlines, Air France, and Delta. A public-private partnership spearheaded by Air France operates Air Côte d'Ivoire, the country's flag carrier.

Abidjan remains one of the most contemporary and livable cities in the region. Its school system is excellent by regional standards. It includes a number of excellent French language- and curriculum-based schools and an international school based on the US curriculum.

ENERGY

As more people migrate to the cities, energy needs increase dramatically. Although exploration teams first discovered natural gas in Côte d'Ivoire in the 1980s, it was not until the mid-1990s that companies began to develop the valuable resource. The country previously imported electricity from Ghana but now produces enough electricity for its own needs and is able to sell electricity to other African countries as well.

Before the discovery of natural gas, the annual production of electricity in the early 1990s totaled about 2 billion kilowatt-hours—much of it generated by hydroelectric installations. Today, Côte d'Ivoire has an 88 percent urban electrification rate, and a 31 percent rural electrification rate. Hydropower, which is renewable, remains one of the country's main sources of electricity, along with natural gas. Ten percent of power production is exported to neighbors.

WORK

The legal minimum working age in Côte d'Ivoire is sixteen, and the Ministry of Employment and Civil Service strictly enforces this provision in the civil service and in multinational companies. There are reports, nevertheless, of adolescents under sixteen being employed in small workshops. A monthly minimum wage, last raised by 60 percent in 2013, is imposed by the government. This rate is enforced for salaried workers employed by the government or registered with the social security office. A slightly higher minimum wage applies to construction workers. The minimum wage varies according to occupation, with the lowest set at $100 (60,000 CFA francs) per month. This meager earning is not enough to provide a decent standard of living for a family. Unfortunately, the majority of the labor force works in agriculture, forestry, or in the informal sector, where minimum wage rules do not apply. The informal sector refers to jobs done without government oversight or tax collection, such as jobs done for cash, work paid for through bartering, or "under the table" employment.

Through the Ministry of Employment and Civil Service, the government enforces a comprehensive labor code governing the terms and conditions of work for wage earners and salaried workers. Those employed in the formal, transparent sector are reasonably protected against unfair compensation, excessive hours, and arbitrary firing. Government labor inspectors can order employers to correct any substandard conditions, and a labor court can levy fines if an employer fails to comply. The labor code grants all citizens, except members of the police, gendarmerie, and military forces, the right to join unions, call strikes, and to bargain collectively.

A new labor code was passed in 2015 that attempts to address seasonal and poorly paid work. It also further strengthens the freedom to unionize and promotes job access for those with special needs. The code also provides for occupational safety and health standards. Nonetheless, in the sprawling informal sector of the economy the government's occupational health and safety regulations are enforced capriciously at best.

INTERNET LINKS

https://www.cocoalife.org/in-the-cocoa-origins/cocoa-life-in-cote-divoire
Learn more about what it takes to grow cocoa in Côte d'Ivoire.

https://www.mcc.gov
This site has everything you need to know about the Millennium Challenge Corporation.

https://www.worldbank.org/en/country/cotedivoire
Check out what the World Bank is doing in Côte d'Ivoire.

ENVIRONMENT

A waterfall flows freely near Man, Côte d'Ivoire.

5

N TODAY'S WORLD, WHICH IS increasingly affected by global warming, the environment has become a touchstone issue for many nations and economies. In order to look toward the future, regions are making long-term plans about how to curb their emissions and deal with potential extreme weather events, among other symptoms of global warming. Countries are also dealing with major biodiversity losses following decades of untethered economic development and agricultural work. In the twenty-first century, no country is immune to environmental issues, and all of them, including Côte d'Ivoire, are being forced to engage in challenging, oftentimes uncomfortable conversations about how they will interact with the environment going forward.

Côte d'Ivoire is particularly rich in flora and fauna. It has the highest level of biodiversity in West Africa, with over 1,200 animal species and 4,700 plant species. Most of this diversity occurs in the country's rugged interior region. At one time, Côte d'Ivoire was home to West Africa's largest rain forests. This prodigious biodiversity, however, is threatened by deforestation.

Since its independence in 1960, Côte d'Ivoire's forested area has fallen from 39.5 million acres (16 million ha) to less than 7.4 million acres (3 million ha), a fate that does not bode well for a country that is so highly dependent on the environment. By some estimates, only 2 percent of the country is now covered by primary forest. More frustrating, the data on the extent and condition of the forest areas are frequently inaccurate and difficult to locate, due in part to a lack of standard classifications for forest types. While many organizations are tracking and working on deforestation, concrete data is limited, which also limits the steps that can be taken.

Côte d'Ivoire has a relatively diversified agricultural economy, thanks to the abundance of natural resources. About two-thirds of the population makes a living farming cocoa (cacao), coffee, palm oil, rubber, pineapples, bananas, and cotton. During the 1960s and 1970s, timber exports were of major economic importance, ranking third behind cocoa and coffee as an export earner. Côte d'Ivoire remains the largest exporter of cocoa in the world. Cocoa farms are one of the biggest culprits when it comes to deforestation. Acres are regularly cleared of trees in order to accommodate new cacao plants. Overexploitation, meanwhile, has depleted many of the country's tropical timber resources.

Unfortunately, Côte d'Ivoire's environmental problems do not end with dwindling timber resources. Another looming peril is water pollution from industrial and agricultural effluents and from raw sewage.

FOREST DEPLETION

Forests play a fundamental role in the basic functioning of the planet. They provide homes and habitats for multitudes of plant and animal species as well as for indigenous human communities. They also serve as a key defense against global warming and are indispensable partners in maintaining soil quality, limiting erosion, stabilizing hillsides, and modulating flooding. When forests

Forest loss has made life more difficult for the people of Côte d'Ivoire who depend on the forests to meet their basic needs. With an economy so reliant on agricultural exports, the challenge facing Côte d'Ivoire is finding ways to continue feeding an ever-growing population without permanently devastating the natural resources base on which all agricultural production hinges. The World Food Programme, or WFP, has been helping to feed the children and families in Côte d'Ivoire since 1968. For children who attend school, WFP provides balanced daily meals, take-home rations, and special nutrient powder to boost nutrition. The WFP also provides assistance for pregnant and nursing women. Through these activities, the program hopes to feed the next generation of Ivorians, ensuring a prosperous future.

are cleared, the soil's physical and chemical properties undergo far-reaching changes, leading to a loss of nutrients, accelerated soil erosion, and falling yields. Like most of West Africa, Côte d'Ivoire has suffered severe deforestation. Slash-and-burn agricultural techniques, uncontrolled fires, mining, and logging for tropical hardwoods are the primary causes of forest loss.

The situation has worsened in the twentieth and twenty-first centuries. For most of the twentieth century, loggers and farmers were turning trees into cash, a process that gave Côte d'Ivoire one of the highest standards of living in Africa. Prior to the outbreak of the first civil war, the Ivorian government devoted serious effort to making conservation a priority. It set aside 17 percent of the country in protected areas and took measures against illegal logging and poaching. The war, however, disabled law and order all across Côte d'Ivoire, allowing illegal loggers to plunder the country's dwindling forest reserves at breakneck rates. Between 1900 and 1980, Côte d'Ivoire's forests disappeared at a rate of 1.5 percent a year. Between 1990 and 2015, that number increased to 4.3 percent per year. In some areas, such as official forest reserves, the rate has reached up to 25 percent in the twenty-first century.

A fluted samba tree is cut by a logger in the Ivorian forest.

If deforestation continues at current rates, experts estimate that natural forests will no longer satisfy the local demand for logs, and that the country will become an importer of timber by the end of the century.

ILLEGAL LOGGING

Trees can take hundreds of years to grow. Unfortunately, in times of war, long-term forest protection policies are abandoned for short-term financial gains. Such was the case in Côte d'Ivoire when a civil war flared up in September 2002. Giant old hardwood trees that were plentiful in the equatorial forests of southern and western Côte d'Ivoire were indiscriminately felled by a number of groups, from pro-government militia chiefs to rebel warlords and timber companies. Even ordinary villagers wanted a piece of the forest. In some cases, there was no one to stop illegal loggers, while in others gangs wielded guns to force their way past forest guards and anyone else who may have tried to stop them. Corruption and poverty also had parts to play. The civil crisis resulted in increasing poverty, and many people in the countryside were so poor that they were willing to do anything for some cash.

Fortunes were certainly made from illegal logging in the freewheeling environment of war-torn Côte d'Ivoire. This has put the governance of the country's remaining natural resources under a lot of pressure.

Although the conflict is officially over and the second civil war has also ended, the country is still in a state of rebuilding, and the future for forest conservation is unclear. Since 2011, the country has been working with the World Bank and other partners on the REDD+ process, which helps establish policies and frameworks to fight against deforestation and reduce emissions at the same time.

THE VOLUNTARY PARTNERSHIP AGREEMENT

President Ouattara and members of his government are aware that illegal logging degrades the environment, hurts the economy, and creates social problems, especially for those who rely on the forest for their everyday needs. Ever since he took office, Ouattara has been working toward a change in forest laws. In February 2013, the president began negotiating a Voluntary Partnership Agreement with the European Union, which seeks to improve forest governance and promote the legal timber trade over illegal business. Under it, Côte d'Ivoire would pledge to develop a system to assure timber legality. Licenses could then be issued to legal timber products. With the licensing process in place, Côte d'Ivoire would export to the EU only these verified legal timber products.

In return, the verified products would enter the EU marketplace without the logistical and legal hassles usually required by EU timber regulations. So far, President Ouattara has worked hard to get all stakeholders involved, including the private sector, indigenous groups, government, and civil society. In 2017, the government began to modernize its policies on forests, agriculture, and land. Though negotiations toward the signed VPA are still in process, both sides hope that a formal agreement can be signed in the coming years.

Wildlife, such as these antelope, abounds in Comoé National Park.

COMOÉ NATIONAL PARK

On April 30, 2009, the World Bank approved the Protected Area Project, providing a grant of $2.54 million to help Côte d'Ivoire improve the management of the habitat and fauna of the Comoé National Park. The park, located in the northeastern region of Côte d'Ivoire, was initially added as a World Heritage Site because of the abounding diversity of plant life present around the Comoé River (also called the Komoé). There are also a large number of mammals in the park, including at least nine monkey species. Because of improper management and continued poaching and overgrazing, the park was added to the list of World Heritage Sites in Danger in 2003. However, it was removed from the list in 2017 following improvements in conservation and habitat management.

The Protected Area Project ensured that there were adequate institutional, financial, and technical capacities in place to sustainably manage the great park. It also reached out to the diverse indigenous park communities—defined as the thousands of people living on the fringes of the site—through its support of public awareness campaigns, biodiversity training, land management contracts, and alternate livelihoods. The project closed at the end of 2014, with a final budget of $2.4 million.

2006 TOXIC WASTE EVENT

Pollution is an ongoing issue in Côte d'Ivoire. Here, a man collects plastic in a canal.

One of the major environmental issues that Côte d'Ivoire faces is water pollution from sewage and industrial and agricultural effluents. Although this contamination has long been a problem in Côte d'Ivoire, a tragedy in 2006 brought the issue to the limelight, resulting in the resignation of a nine-month-old transitional government led by Prime Minister Charles Konan Banny.

The dumping of 560 tons (508 metric tons) of toxic material in fourteen open-air sites in Abidjan in 2006 led to the death of seventeen people and widespread sickness. The toxic waste scandal focused a spotlight on the ways dangerous substances move around the globe, particularly between developed and developing countries.

This lethal waste was a mixture of oil residue and caustic soda used to rinse out the tanks of a Greek-owned cargo ship operating for a Dutch-based company, Trafigura. Investigations showed that the material was spread, allegedly by subcontractors, across the city and surrounding areas, dumped in waste grounds, public dumps, and along roads in populated areas. The sludge caused nausea, rashes, fainting, diarrhea, and headaches that affected tens of thousands of people. Almost one hundred thousand Ivorians sought medical attention for the effects of these dumped chemicals.

Directly following the disaster, the United Nations sent its UN Environment team of experts to monitor the affected sites. Sadly, all of the environmental monitoring systems that the UN Environment built directly following the 2006 event were lost during the violence of 2010—2011, so years of monitoring data have been lost.

At the request of the Ivorian government, UN Environment was invited in 2018 to Côte d'Ivoire to complete an independent scientific environmental audit of the sites affected by the toxic waste dumping. Four international experts took samples of soil, water, air, fruits, vegetables, and more from eighteen different sites. One hundred thirty samples were collected altogether. Results of the study found that none of the sites where waste was dumped showed contamination exceeding limits set by the Ivorian government, and also found that none of the sites required additional intervention. However, some of

Côte d'Ivoire is home to a spectacular coastline that features pristine beaches, wildlife, residential areas, ports, and industrial zones. In recent years, the coast has become more vulnerable to oil spills, as oil ships move along a route adjacent to the coastline. Many of these ships carry stolen or illegal oil and are not regulated by law, making them more susceptible to spills. Additionally, oil production in the region, including offshore drilling, continues to grow at a clip.

The National Committee for Disaster Management has yet to take up the creation of a new oil-spill response plan, putting its coastline at risk. An oil spill would impact fishing ports, tourism, and local communities. Advocates are working hard to get the word out about the increased risk and need for planning.

the samples showed that a few of the official municipal waste disposal sites, including one at Akouédo, needed to be decommissioned or closely monitored due to elevated levels of air and groundwater pollution, and even some slightly elevated levels of pollution in vegetables grown on site.

INTERNET LINKS

http://climate.org/deforestation-and-climate-change
This Climate Institute page gives an in-depth look at the relationship between deforestation and climate change.

http://www.euredd.efi.int/cotedivoire
The REDD+ page breaks down Côte d'Ivoire's deforestation challenges and opportunities.

https://www.unenvironment.org/explore-topics/disasters -conflicts/where-we-work/cote-divoire
The United Nations Environment Program gives a detailed report on outcomes following the 2006 disaster.

https://www.usaid.gov/cote-divoire/environment
USAID is present in Côte d'Ivoire in many sectors, including the environment.

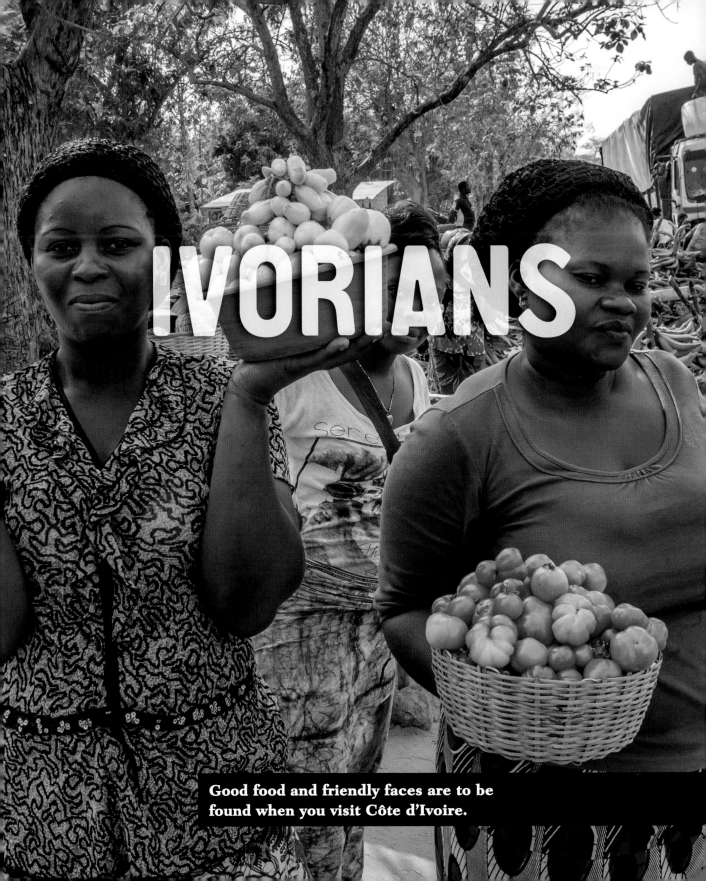

IVORIANS

Good food and friendly faces are to be found when you visit Côte d'Ivoire.

WHEN VISITING A NEW COUNTRY, you might wonder about the people who live there. Will they have the same customs and values as you do? Will they be easy to talk to? What will they wear? Luckily, even though people in different parts of the world have their own unique characteristics, they are still people. They want friends, jobs, safety, and good health. They care about their families and about building a good future for their children. Ivorians are no different.

The population of Côte d'Ivoire is made up of many different groups of people. The majority are the indigenous people, who come from different ethnic groups, the largest of which is the Baule. Ivorians consider respect for one's family and elders to be very important. They are generally a warm and hospitable people. In some parts of the country, especially in rural areas, some aspects of Ivorian culture—food, religion, dress, and daily life—have remained unchanged for hundreds of years. People continue to practice the folkways of their ancestors. Nonetheless, there has been a momentous shift in social identity. Ivorians now consider themselves citizens of Côte d'Ivoire first, then as members of their ethnic groups.

POPULATION

Côte d'Ivoire has about twenty-six million people, with an annual growth rate of 2.3 percent (2018 estimate), one of the highest in the world. Nearly 60 percent of the population is under the age of twenty-five, and the fertility rate is about 3.5 children per woman, which means it is likely that the country will continue to see high growth rates in the youth sector for years to come. The median age is nineteen years old.

MANY ETHNIC GROUPS

Côte d'Ivoire is a diverse cultural puzzle with over sixty ethnic groups. The major groups came relatively recently from neighboring countries—the Malinke people came after the collapse of the Mali Empire in the sixteenth century; the Kru people migrated from Liberia around 1600; and the Senufo and Lobi tribes moved southward from Burkina Faso and Mali. It was not until the eighteenth

A Senufo group performs a traditional panther dance.

Across Côte d'Ivoire, about three out of ten adolescents (aged fifteen to nineteen) have begun to have children. Official law sets the minimum age for marriage at eighteen years old for women, but about a third of women get married before their eighteenth birthday. Twelve percent are married before the age of fifteen. This young marriage age, combined with limited access to health care and a recent history of conflict, have resulted in a contraceptive use rate that hovers around 12 percent for adolescents. Young women simply do not have the access and education they need in order to plan their own families.

In an effort to slow this birth rate among teenagers, the government has launched several campaigns and initiatives, including the Zero Pregnancy at School campaign. In 2016, the Ministry of Health partnered with other organizations to host a national workshop on youth reproductive health. Unfortunately, these efforts often fail to address rural and out-of-school youth, who often lack even the most basic information and services.

century that the Akan people—the Baule, Anyi, and Abron—migrated from Ghana into the eastern and central areas of the country. At around the same time, the Dyula moved from Guinea into the northwest. The vast ebb and flow of African clans has left a rich trail of languages and customs.

BAULE is the largest ethnic group in Côte d'Ivoire, making up 15 to 20 percent of the country's population. They are a subgroup of the Akan peoples, who form 28.8 percent of the population. The Baule live in the central part of the country, where they primarily farm cocoa, yams, and maize. They have a centralized government with a king or a chief at the top, as well as subchiefs. For the Baule, religion is a mixture of ancestor worship and nature gods, which are often represented in sculpture.

THE ANYI AND ABRON The Anyi, also called the Agni, are a subgroup of the Akan that migrated to Côte d'Ivoire in the eighteenth century, fleeing the Ashanti. Their economy is primarily agricultural, centered around the production of banana and taro. As with other indigenous groups, markets are run every four days and are the center of the economy. The Anyi live in loose neighborhoods and have their own titled officials. The Abron people are another subgroup of the Akan.

THE SENUFO The Senufo people populate not only Côte d'Ivoire but also Ghana, Burkina Faso, and southern Mali. They practice agriculture and hunting. Most members of the Senufo group are farmers or artisans, and they produce a variety of sculptures in their small villages. A central religious idea is a feminine spirit known as an "ancient mother" or "ancient woman," who guides the society. There are four subgroups within the culture: Poro, Sandogo, Wambele, and Tyekpa. These groups create their own art and fill different roles in the government and education sectors.

THE DAN, OR YAKUBA, tribe is one of the most interesting tribes in the country. The word *yakuba* in the local dialect means "all that begins by animated discussion." The Dan are noted for their dance masks, and dances are performed to mark all the important life events. Besides masks, the Dan are also renowned for other crafts, including woven cloth, wooden spoons, and murals painted on exterior house walls.

THE DYULA live in the far northwest. They came from Guinea, bringing with them the Islamic faith. In addition to trading, their major activity, the Dyula are subsistence farmers of rice, millet (a grain), and peanuts. They also keep goats, sheep, poultry, and some cattle. This is a patrilineal society, with the oldest male as head of his lineage. Villages tend to be grouped around men with the same clan name, and headmen are called imams, or religious leaders.

A blend of Islam and traditional beliefs has resulted in healing and magic becoming very important. Holy men are called on for protective charms or the invocation of a curse on an enemy.

THE LOBI This group migrated from Ghana to Burkina Faso around 1770 and then moved into Côte d'Ivoire over the next hundred years. They came in search of uncultivated lands for farming. Today, they continue to practice subsistence

Côte d'Ivoire cooperates with the United Nations High Commissioner for Refugees (UNHCR) in health, education, and food distribution programs for refugees. Following the outbreak of the Liberian civil war, which killed 10 percent of its 2.5 million people and displaced 700,000 others, many sought refuge in Côte d'Ivoire. When the civil war broke out in Côte d'Ivoire in 2002, these exiles were in imminent danger because anti-Liberian sentiments had hit an all-time high. These refugees were targeted by the military and armed youths who accused them of being associated with antigovernment forces. Thousands of Liberians were made homeless as security forces set their houses on fire.

Today, relations between the two countries have calmed. In September 2017, Liberia and Côte d'Ivoire signed an agreement reflecting a new cooperating relationship between the two countries.

farming and also raise livestock for trading, dowries, and offerings. The head of a Lobi community is known as *thil*. Artisans within the communities make both everyday objects and religious figures.

THE KULANGO are closely related to the Lobi, their former enemies. The two tribes occupy the same region and share similar languages, customs, lifestyles, and religious beliefs. The Kulango are primarily farmers, growing crops such as yams, corn, peanuts, cotton, and watermelons. Some of them also breed goats, sheep, and cattle. The women gather wild fruits and nuts, whereas the men do most of the agricultural work.

Each Kulango village is made up of several small settlements of mud huts. The huts are clustered around a center court, which serves as a meeting place. Every settlement consists of several extended families, each of which is its own economic unit.

THE KRU have a long association with the sea. Fishing has long been their major activity, though it is now declining. Traditionally, the men loaded logging ships and made long sea passages with their cargoes. The Kru have tried to maintain their autonomy, but this has proved difficult, and they are

While it is not illegal to be lesbian, gay, bisexual, or transgender in Côte d'Ivoire, the country still has a long way to go when it comes to acceptance. Unlike many British colonies, Côte d'Ivoire did not inherit laws against LGBTQ behavior from France. However, same-sex couples are not recognized by the government and are not eligible to get married or adopt children. There are no antidiscrimination laws on the books, and people do not have the right to change their legal gender.

According to the 2011 Human Rights Report, while there is no official discrimination in employment, housing, or other sectors, there is widespread social stigmatization of LGBTQ people. Gay men have reportedly experienced beatings, abuse, and extortion by police and members of the military. There are very few LGBTQ organizations active within the country, and those that are there act with great caution.

becoming more assimilated into the Ivorian mainstream. Nevertheless, their traditional oral culture, accounting for numerous folk stories and morality tales, remains strong.

NON-IVORIANS

Non-Ivorian Africans who reside in Côte d'Ivoire number about five million. They come from Burkina Faso, Ghana, Guinea, Mali, Nigeria, Liberia, and elsewhere.

There are also a number of other foreigners living in Côte d'Ivoire, including some Lebanese and French. Many Protestant missionaries from the United States and Canada also reside in the nation. During the first and second Ivorian civil wars, missionaries and other foreigners were evacuated from Côte d'Ivoire. Some were placed in neighboring countries, while others were sent home.

ECONOMIC INEQUALITY

From the 1960s to 1980s, there was a wide gap between the ruling elite and those who were ruled. The wealthy, urban, and educated privileged minority received most of the benefits and had access to the country's resources. Political appointments were typically accompanied by land concessions in Abidjan. This resulted in a scarcity of building lots and high rents for everyone else. Cabinet ministers got monthly housing allowances and lived in relative luxury. Personal wealth and government service became closely linked. For ordinary people who lived in rural areas, secondary education and access to health care were nonexistent. Employment was a very significant indicator of social status. Government employees earned far more than the national average, whereas many people were unemployed in the countryside. In general, the difference in the daily lives of the urban elite and the poor majority was enormous.

Since the 1990s there have been some changes in this state of affairs. The middle class is expanding as the living standards of low-wage workers rise. Opportunities for social mobility are slowly increasing. Regrettably, the living conditions of the very poor have changed little, and they remain alienated from the overall economic progress of the country. Troublesome and serious inequalities in the distribution of wealth persist.

INTERNET LINKS

http://www.mappery.com/Ivory-Coast-Tribal-Map
This map gives an overview of the historic locations of indigenous groups in Côte d'Ivoire.

https://minorityrights.org/country/cote-divoire
Minority Rights Group International works to protect ethnic minorities throughout the world.

LIFESTYLE

Many people make their living by fishing the waters off the coast of Côte d'Ivoire.

7

N OW THAT WE LIVE IN A CONNECTED, globalized world, young Ivorians know all about the lives that people lead across the world, and they are more able than ever before to dream and work toward their goals. Whether they are part of the 50 percent of the population that lives in an urban center, or the half that lives in a rural setting, youth are having a big impact on Côte d'Ivoire, changing the face of education, health care, family life, and so much more.

In much of sub-Saharan Africa, people dwell in rural communities, but in Côte d'Ivoire, a little over half the population lives in cities. Increasingly, young people, mostly men, are drawn to the cities where they believe they will find a better standard of living. Additionally, deforestation is making the land too barren to grow crops. Some families quit the countryside and head to the bustling urban centers. The most popular destinations are Abidjan and Bouaké. Abidjan has a population of nearly 5 million people. The capital, Yamoussoukro, has around 231,000 residents.

Unfortunately, movement from the country to the city does not always mean economic prosperity. As of 2015, 46.3 percent of Ivorian residents were living below the poverty line. In addition, there is massive population displacement and rising unemployment. In 2013, the unemployment

Ivorian families come in many different shapes and sizes.

rate stood just under 10 percent. But one thing is certain: whether Ivorians are living in the countryside or in the cities, the traditions of hospitality, family, and kinship are loyally sustained.

FAMILY

In Côte d'Ivoire, the extended family is the basic social unit. The family is linked to a larger society through clans, called lineages, traced through male or female descent. An entire village is frequently made up of one single clan. Older members teach the young the history of their clan and enable them to cultivate a sense of social responsibility.

Every child born is a child of the entire village, and the child's success or failure is felt by everyone in the village. The responsibility to raise children and teach them social values belongs to everyone. This connection to others is of paramount importance. It is instilled at an early age, so that even if people leave the village, they will always act in the knowledge that they are a representative of their family and village. Thus they should never bring disgrace on those still at home. This reinforces the vital concept of community above self.

WOMEN

Traditionally, a woman's role is to be a wife and mother. Boys are taught from an early age to always respect girls because one day the girls will be wives and mothers. Taking care of the family budget and the children, particularly the girls, is the woman's responsibility. In Ivorian society, the relationship between a mother and her daughter is a very special one because they spend a great deal of time together.

In rural settings, a woman is also expected to perform most of the less physical farming tasks, such as growing the vegetables, feeding the animals, and taking goods to the market. For the fortunate women who can afford to attend school and complete their education, there are rosier opportunities.

An increasing number of women are employed in important sectors of the economy, such as medicine, business, and university teaching.

Politically, women are also getting more opportunities. In 2012, Niale Kaba was named finance minister, the first woman to hold the job since the nation gained independence. Massandji Toure-Litse is also head of the cocoa marketing board, one of the most important roles for the country's cocoa-based economy. In 2018, Côte d'Ivoire became the second country to launch the African Women Leaders Network, a group that hopes to catapult more women into leadership positions in African countries, where they can help build the future for their nations.

EDUCATION

Educational services expanded considerably after independence. During the 1970s, the educational system in Côte d'Ivoire was the envy of other African countries. The government had heavily subsidized education and even experimented with televised lessons, one of the few African nations to do so. The recession in the 1980s, however, led to cutbacks in funding. Political instability has also resulted in the halting of educational system development as many schools were closed in areas occupied by rebel forces. The quality of teaching dropped sharply, especially at the primary level, owing to the lack of qualified teachers. Today, only about 55 percent of children attend primary school. The rest stay home, help their parents, or work in agriculture.

School is free of charge and officially mandatory between the ages of six and sixteen, although this rule is not strictly enforced. In general, there is poor access to education, especially for girls, which leads to low rates of literacy and a lack of skilled adult workers. A lack of education has also been shown to contribute to adolescent pregnancy and the prevalence of HIV/AIDS. Elementary school lasts for six years. However, many children leave school at an early age, particularly girls and those living in rural areas. Children have to work on the farm as soon as they are old enough to do chores. For many, helping out the family takes priority over school. There are also insufficient resources for those who do want to attend school. A dearth of teachers, school

"Women still aren't entirely free today. Education is the big problem for girls, because parents prefer to educate the boys first."
—Fofanan Man, 2016

Ivorian children attend school in a village in 2018.

buildings, and quality teaching contributes to parents' lack of motivation to send their children to school. For children who enter school, there is about a 52 percent chance that they will reach fifth grade.

By working beside their parents instead of attending school, children learn from an early age the values of their family and village. Girls are taught by their mothers, and boys mostly talk with their fathers and other males. When the girls get married and leave home, the responsibility of taking care of the elderly family members falls on the sons. Rather than telling children what to do or not to do, Ivorian parents get their message across by reciting simple stories with morals that have been handed down from generation to generation—delightful fables with a punch.

For those who continue their education, after four years of secondary education, students take exams. If they perform well, they get a certificate.

After that, another three years is spent studying for the secondary school certificate required to enter a university.

There are several universities in Côte d'Ivoire. One of the most popular is the Université Alassane Ouattara, a public school founded in 1992 and renamed in 2012. It is located in Bouaké. Students there can study medicine, management, communication, economics, the environment, and more. A polytechnical institute is located in Yamoussoukro, and several other universities and colleges can be found in Abidjan.

A sign marks the entrance to a university in Abidjan.

Founded in 1959, the National University of Côte d'Ivoire enrolled students in college programs for many years, and the programs were subsidized by the French government. Unfortunately, the institution was used as a military base during several conflicts and civil wars, and remains closed.

The literacy rate of Côte d'Ivoire is 43.1 percent. This is slightly lower than the regional average, though it is significantly lower than the world average. Although elementary education is compulsory, this requirement is not effectively enforced. The government is aware that its national literacy rate is not acceptable. A system in which many children, particularly girls and rural youngsters, do not go to school at all is lamentable. This situation is slowly changing as the political situation stabilizes following the 2010—2011 civil war.

After the second civil war, Côte d'Ivoire set to rebuilding educational opportunities for children and youth. While about 50 percent of children do not attend school despite mandatory education for kids ages six to sixteen, there are plans in place to improve access as well as quality of education. In 2012, the country implemented a three-year Transitional Education Plan, which was then extended through 2016. In May 2017, Côte d'Ivoire's government adopted a ten-year Education and Training Sector Plan. The plan was built in collaboration with the Global Partnership for Education. It addresses illiteracy, vocational programs, access, educating young women, early childhood development, and much more.

MEN

An Ivorian man is brought up, first and foremost, to provide for his wife and family. An ability to do this well results in higher social status for the individual.

The last thirty years have seen many young men leaving their villages to seek better lives in the cities, where there are more job opportunities and they can earn more money. This migration has brought about many social problems. Most young men find life in the cities to be very different from life at home. In a village, for instance, it is perfectly natural to eat with any family and stay in any hut, but in the cities one must pay for food and lodging. If the young man is poor, he will have to depend on relatives who live there.

Greetings in Côte d'Ivoire are warm and friendly. Here, musicians greet each other with a handshake.

CHARACTER

Respect for one's family, elderly people, and women is a distinctive quality of Ivorians. Ivorians are very hospitable people—they are always ready to welcome strangers into their homes for some food and drink. They are also extremely polite and really enjoy inquiring about a visitor's health and family. Ivorians are a gentle and relaxed people. To the Ivorian, trust is very important in a relationship, whether one of business or friendship. Without trust, nothing much gets done.

CUSTOMS

In the traditional Ivorian greeting, it is important to inquire about a person's health, family, work, or the weather. Getting down to the business at hand immediately in any encounter is considered rude. Women do not shake hands with each other but instead kiss each other three times on the cheeks, starting with the left cheek and alternating sides. Men, however, typically shake hands. At social functions, it is appropriate for men to shake hands with everyone when entering and again when leaving. Eye contact is usually avoided, particularly between father and child. It is considered extremely rude to stare at other people. Giving gifts is important, especially to those who are higher in the social hierarchy or are respected people. For example, if a mother-in-law comes for a visit, she would expect a gift. The thinking behind giving presents is that if God has been good to you, then you should be happy to spread that good fortune around.

CLOTHING

Ivorians place great importance on clothing. Their clothing can be divided into two types—traditional and casual attire. Traditional formal dress for men is pants and shirt beneath a long, embroidered robe that reaches to the ground. Their more casual clothes resemble Western-style pajamas. For women, traditional dress is also a long, embroidered robe. For daily wear, a woman may put on a loose blouse and wrap a piece of colorful cloth around her waist for a skirt. In our globalized economy and interconnected world, global fashion and shopping are becoming more accessible to Ivorians. In 2017, the Afrik Fashion Show, part of the annual Africa Fashion Week, was held in Abidjan.

Well-known wedding customs such as flowers and white dresses are popular in Côte d'Ivoire.

EVENTS

Ceremonies, whether happy or sad, are an integral part of Ivorian society. Special events, such as births, weddings, and funerals, are given great attention. A birth is usually celebrated for one to two days. If the family is Christian, the child is baptized. Guests give the parents a gift, which is usually a small amount of money, and after the church ceremony, everyone gathers for a feast.

Marriage is an important social institution, providing continuity and cohesion in society, and it is always an occasion for great joy and celebration. While weddings in urban centers are becoming more Westernized, many indigenous groups practice their own traditional wedding rituals. Polygamy, although outlawed in 1964, is still an accepted lifestyle among some ethnic groups.

DAILY LIFE

About half the Ivorian population is urban, and many people live in dense areas in Abidjan and Bouaké. Urban centers attract large numbers of rural migrants, who come either as permanent settlers or as short-term workers. In 2018, the population growth rate for the country on the whole was 2.3 percent. There are considerably more amenities in the cities of Abidjan and Bouaké, where many rich people live, than in smaller towns. The standard of living in Côte d'Ivoire's cities is higher than in most African countries.

However, daily life for the average young man looking for work and trying to survive can be tough. Although Côte d'Ivoire is making some small progress in lifting its overall standard of living, health services, and literacy, there is always room for improvement. Since the end of the civil conflict in 2011, the country has received a bump in foreign investment and economic growth, partially spurred by continued demand for chocolate and palm oil. The IMF and World Bank announced in 2012 that they would be offering Côte d'Ivoire about $4 billion in debt relief. With continued economic opportunity, there is hope for a brighter future for the men, women, and families of Côte d'Ivoire.

CITIES

Despite advancement in opportunities, many urban Ivorians live in slums due to high populations and the high poverty rate. Slums are crowded, generally unkempt neighborhoods. In 2015, it was reported that about 56 percent of urban residents in Côte d'Ivoire lived in areas that could be considered "slums."

Many people also live with their extended family. In fact, Ivorians have long embraced their duty to care for their extended family. When a nuclear family living in the city is joined by their cousins and nephews from the countryside, their small rented apartment becomes very cramped. Nevertheless, the head of the household usually pays all the bills if he has a job and allows his cousins and nephews, or any relative in need, to stay for free at his house.

RURAL LIFE

Rural living features in Côte d'Ivoire vary among locations and the clans. Generally, each village consists of several small settlements. The settlements include a number of mud huts with cone-shaped roofs made of palm leaves, although corrugated metal is now more frequently used. Dwellings are clustered around a central open area that is often used as a gathering place. The Senufo live in villages of circular huts with unusual, elaborately carved wooden doors.

A typical day for a rural family begins early. Rising at about 4 a.m., the men are the first to go to their land and start working. The women must first clean their hut, get fires burning, and look after the children. Then they join their husbands later in the morning, taking care of the vegetable crops, such as peppers, potatoes, and peanuts. The men are responsible for clearing land of trees and brush so that yams, bananas, or other crops can be planted.

Farming is hard work. The farmers have to spend long hours under the scorching sun. The women return home around midafternoon to tend to their children and to cook the family's dinner. For the men, the day ends when the sun sets.

Some rural residents regularly collect branches in order to heat their homes.

HEALTH

Health services in Côte d'Ivoire were comparatively good before the late 1980s. The economic crisis, however, made it extremely hard for the government and burdened medics to meet the needs of a rapidly growing population. In the 1990s, the ratio of Ivorians to doctors was 17,847 to 1. In 2002, the civil war severely disrupted health-care services in the northern part of the country. Some health facilities were destroyed, and many medical personnel fled the region. Those who remained were concentrated in urban areas for the sake of their security. Thankfully, many such medical personnel have since returned to their deserted health stations.

Western-style hospitals are located in Abidjan, Bouaké, Daloa, and Korhogo, and clinics can be found in other areas. There are also many practitioners of indigenous forms of medicine.

Chronic malnutrition, resulting in stunted growth and other afflictions, is one of the most serious health problems for young children in the country. Children in rural areas are twice as likely to be underweight as those in the cities. There

Mother-Child Hospital opened in a suburb of Abidjan in 2018.

are also high incidences of tuberculosis and malaria, as well as communicable diseases like cholera, typhoid fever, and foodborne illness. Poor management of waste and sanitation facilities are the main causes of communicable disease.

Côte d'Ivoire remained Ebola-free during the 2014 outbreak of the virus that left thousands dead in nearby Liberia, Guinea, and Sierra Leone, thanks to an effective public-awareness campaign and a temporary ban on travel from the affected countries. However, while Ebola is not currently an issue in the country, there is always a risk that the virus could cross the borders into Côte d'Ivoire, and the national capacities for prevention and response do need to be strengthened.

Noncommunicable diseases such as cancer and high blood pressure are on the rise due to late diagnosis and management, as well as lifestyle changes. Thirty-one percent of deaths in the country are due to noncommunicable diseases.

The year 2016 marked the first year of a five-year National Health Development Plan, which has its sights set on high standards of health across the country, especially in areas where people are now the most poor and vulnerable. The World Health Organization has helped Côte d'Ivoire develop national policies and plans in the past and is committed to a continued partnership as the country moves toward its new goals.

The Ivorian life expectancy at birth is fifty-eight years for males and sixty-two years for females.

Since the late 1990s, HIV/AIDS has been a rapidly expanding problem, but many organizations are working hard to reverse this course. Today, the country has the second-highest HIV prevalence rate in West Africa, at 3.7 percent. HIV/AIDS is highly concentrated among females, adolescents, and children. In 2016, the Joint United Nations Team on AIDS renewed its response to the epidemic, working to end AIDS in Côte d'Ivoire by 2030. They continue to face challenges such as low medication coverage for children living with HIV, a lack

HIV/AIDS ADVANCES

One of the most significant achievements in the fight against HIV/AIDS in Côte d'Ivoire has been in work to eliminate mother-to-child transmission. Through training and hiring community health workers, about 80 percent of HIV-positive pregnant and breastfeeding women now have access to the vital medications they need. Programs have been put in place to educate women about HIV, and fully 100 percent of children who tested positive before the age of one have begun treatment. Hospitals now offer more comprehensive pediatric HIV treatment and have formalized recommended protocols for caring for HIV-positive mothers and children.

of community interventions to reduce new infections, a lack of innovative prevention strategies, and lack of identification of those infected. However, the Joint Team worked to provide both the advocacy and technical support needed to form a National HIV Strategic Plan 2016—2020, which will guide national policies and education programs. President Ouattara and First Lady Dominique Ouattara have been vocal about their commitments to wiping out HIV/AIDS and have put dollars behind their words. The president promised to increase domestic funding for the AIDS response by 400 percent in 2017.

INTERNET LINKS

https://www.cdc.gov/globalhivtb/where-we-work/cotedivoire/cotedivoire.html
The Centers for Disease Control and Prevention offers information on disease prevention in Côte d'Ivoire.

https://www.globalpartnership.org
The Global Partnership for Education works to increase access to and quality of education in developing countries.

https://www.who.int/en
The World Health Organization monitors health outcomes in countries around the world.

RELIGION

The Basilica of Our Lady of Peace is topped with a breathtaking blue dome.

CÔTE D'IVOIRE IS HOME TO A MIX OF different religions. From Christianity and Islam to atheism and indigenous religions, beliefs are many. The 2016 constitution builds on a long history of freedom of religious belief and freedom of worship, preventing religious discrimination in employment. In fact, the government continues to intentionally include both Muslim and Christian religious leaders in political reconciliation and electoral efforts. A March 2016 terrorist attack in Grand-Bassam was allegedly carried out by a group of Islamist extremists, and that has led to some suspicion and prejudice toward Muslims across the country. This is just one of the many challenges the country has faced as it tries to live out the tenets of a truly religiously open and tolerant system.

8

Peace is the dominant theme in Islam. Peace with Allah, with one's soul, with the family and friends, and with all living creatures. To disturb the peace of anyone or any creature in any shape or form is strictly prohibited.

According to the 2014 census, about 42 percent of those in Côte d'Ivoire are Muslim. Thirty-four percent are Christian. About 4 percent practice indigenous religions as their main affiliation. Some Muslims and Christians also practice some forms of indigenous religion.

MUSLIMS

Islam was founded by the Prophet Muhammad. Born in 570 CE, he left Mecca, Saudi Arabia, in 610 and traveled while preaching his divine revelations.

After Muhammad's death in 632, his followers collected his revelations, putting them into a book called the Quran. This became the holy scripture of Islam. Another book was also compiled—the Hadith, which is a collection of Muhammad's sayings. These beloved observations were memorized and preserved by his companions. Muslims view the Hadith as an additional source of spiritual guidance, besides the Quran. There are several denominations or creeds within Islam, though most Ivorians are Sunni. Sufism is also widespread, and there are some Shia.

There are five primary religious obligations that each Muslim must fulfill in his or her lifetime. They are called the Five Pillars of Islam. Shahadah (sha-HAHD-ah) is the profession of faith. Salat (sa-LAHT) is prayer; Muslims pray five times a day—at dawn, noon, midafternoon, sunset, and nightfall. Zakat (za-KAHT) means almsgiving, or giving up one's surplus wealth. Sawm (sa-AHM) is fasting during religious holidays, like Ramadan. Hajj (HAHJ) means pilgrimage; it is the duty of every Muslim who is fit and can afford it to make at least one pilgrimage to Mecca, Muhammad's birthplace.

MUSLIM HOUSES OF WORSHIP

Muslims worship Allah in a building called a mosque. The early mosques looked like the courtyard of Muhammad's house, the place where the first Muslims gathered to listen to his sermons.

Muslims gather to pray in Abidjan during the Eid al-Adha festival.

POLITICS AND RELIGION

Although the country's political conflicts lay along ethnic rather than religious lines, political and religious affiliations tend to follow ethnic lines—hence some religious groups have been especially hard hit by the civil wars. For instance, many northern ethnic groups are Muslim, and as a result, many Muslims were assumed to be rebels and rebel sympathizers by the government during the civil war and were targeted as suspects.

Fortunately, strong efforts by religious and civil society groups have helped prevent the political crises from turning into religious conflict, but there still survives some societal discrimination against Muslims and followers of traditional indigenous religions.

The design of mosques evolved from very simple to complex structures in a short time. The addition of minarets, or towers from which the calls to prayer are made, was inspired by other religious buildings. The idea of adorning mosques was copied from churches, and some mosques are very beautiful, with decorative calligraphy and depictions of flowers and geometric shapes. Over time, Muslims started to add rooms to mosques to use for travelers, the ill, classes for boys learning the Quran, a library, or a special room for praying women. A fountain or other facility is present so worshippers can wash their hands for purification before prayer. When entering a mosque, a visitor must take off his shoes. Entering a mosque has to be done with the right foot first, while reciting blessings to Muhammad and his family. A person inside a mosque will talk softly so that he does not disturb worshippers who are praying.

A tall minaret towers above the Plateau Mosque in Abidjan.

Although it is considered more meritorious to pray in a mosque with other people, a Muslim may pray almost anywhere—in the fields, offices, factories, or universities. The Friday prayer or sermon at a mosque is considered to be compulsory for all male Muslims.

In 2006, several of the mosques in Côte d'Ivoire's northern region were added to the "tentative" list of UNESCO World Heritage Sites. The "Sudanese" style, developed after the sixteenth century, is found in twenty mosques in Côte d'Ivoire. While they have not yet made it to the official list of World Heritage Sites, they remain beautiful and culturally significant.

CHRISTIANS

Christianity is Côte d'Ivoire's second most widespread religion. Today, Christian subgroups found in the country include the Roman Catholic Church; the Jehovah's Witnesses; the Seventh-Day Adventist Church; the Southern Baptist Church; the Coptic Christians; and the Church of Jesus Christ of Latter-Day Saints, or Mormons. Catholics make up 17.2 percent of the entire population, while those who identify as Evangelical make up 11.8 percent.

Roman Catholicism in Côte d'Ivoire was introduced by French missionaries during the colonial period, particularly among the Anyi people. In general, Roman Catholicism is practiced by the middle class and urban south. Villages adopt certain patron saints and honor them on secular and religious holidays. The Catholic mission in Côte d'Ivoire was established in 1895, but the first African priest was not ordained until 1934. In the 1980s, the church started seminaries and schools throughout the country, and a large cathedral, Saint Paul's, was built in Abidjan. At the same time, President Félix Houphouët-Boigny funded the building of the Basilica of Our Lady of Peace in Yamoussoukro. Completed in 1990 and styled after the Basilica of Saint Peter in Rome, Italy, it is often cited as the world's largest church.

The largest and oldest Protestant denomination in the country is known as Harrism. Founded in 1914 by a Liberian named William Harris, Harrism is now considered more an African religion than a Western one taught by white missionaries. Traveling through Ghana and Côte d'Ivoire, Harris led a simple life. He attracted followers by preaching against adultery, theft, and lying, and condemning excessive wealth.

CHRISTIAN HOUSES OF WORSHIP

In Côte d'Ivoire, Christians worship in buildings called churches. There are several well-known churches in the country today.

BASILICA OF OUR LADY OF PEACE The basilica, situated in Félix Houphouët-Boigny's birthplace, Yamoussoukro, sits on a massive 7.4-acre (3 ha) plaza with a marble Roman-style entrance. It cost $400 million to build, and the

The Church of Jesus Christ of Latter-Day Saints, also known as the Mormon Church or LDS, is heavily focused on global missionary activities. Young people within the church serve two-year missions as a rite of passage. They could be sent anywhere in the world—and some are sent to Côte d'Ivoire. The LDS mission in Abidjan is very small, with just a few missionaries, and many come from neighboring African countries rather than the United States. During the 2010–2011 civil war, LDS missionaries were sent out of Côte d'Ivoire for their own safety. Since then, the church has renewed its attempts to evangelize within the country. In 2018, it announced the opening of a new mission base in Yamoussoukro.

maintenance costs are in the millions of dollars today. With a towering cross on top, it claims to be the largest church in the world. In September 1990, Pope John Paul II visited Côte d'Ivoire for the third time and consecrated the basilica. Since then, it has been visited by millions of people and is a pilgrimage stop for many Catholics around the world.

The floor space of Our Lady of Peace is enormous—it can hold three hundred thousand people. The cathedral has thirty-six beautiful stained-glass windows, the glass all handblown in France. All the figures depicted in the windows are Caucasian except for one solitary black pilgrim, who resembles Houphouët-Boigny. He is portrayed kneeling at the feet of Christ.

SAINT PAUL'S CATHEDRAL is an attractive modern cathedral with a big tower that affords a panoramic view of the city of Abidjan. It was designed by an Italian architect, Aldo Spirito, and consecrated by Pope John Paul II in 1985.

INDIGENOUS RELIGION

Many Ivorians, especially those living in rural areas, continue to follow traditional religions involving ancestor worship. Each ethnic group has its own distinctive religious practices, but some elements are common to all. All the traditional religions are animistic, which means that people believe everything has a soul. They also accept the notions of a supreme being and reincarnation. Besides the creator, there are numerous lesser gods that Ivorians pray to for

A tribal dance is performed by a group of Dan, or Yakuba, people.

good health, bountiful harvests, and the blessing of many children, and whom they honor in village celebrations.

They worship ancestral spirits also, believing in their protective oversight. Ancestral spirits are those members of the family or lineage who have died and transformed into spirits. They remain in constant contact with the living. Through various rituals, the living kin seek their blessings and protection. The principal role of the ancestral spirits is to protect the tribe. The spirits are the real owners of the land—the villagers cannot sell it or they would incur the wrath of their forebears. Magic is also commonly practiced in traditional rites. Good magic keeps the evil spirits safely away. Medicine men dispense charms, tell fortunes, and give advice on how to avoid danger. They also bless gris-gris, which are charmed necklaces that ward off specific evils. If the gris-gris has not been blessed by the medicine man, it won't work.

The Senufo religious leaders, or *marabous*, officiate at ceremonies, honor the gods, and advise people on how to cope with their problems. Sometimes they act as doctors because many illnesses are thought to have spiritual causes.

The Anyi and Baule have a single supreme god or creator figure, Nyame, and a number of subordinate gods who inhabit trees, water, and animals. Below them are still lesser deities whose power is invoked through protective charms. The ancestral spirits who affect the people's daily lives are always in contact with the living and can directly influence a person's fortunes in his present life. Thus it is important for the living to seek their blessings and protection through various rituals. Ancestral spirits are always consulted, sometimes even offered food and drink. Failure to perform such rites makes the spirits angry and can result in misfortune.

The Kru believe in a second god besides the creator. This god is a devil who works against the creator, resulting in humans having a balance of good and evil within themselves. The crux is to maintain this balance of the antagonistic features in their daily lives.

The Dyula believe that their god created the world and four sets of twins. These eight twins were commanded to populate the world and to teach their children to grow crops.

The Lobi think of divination as a means of determining death, disease, or any misfortune. Diviners act like counselors, not predicting the future but suggesting some action to help people cope with their problems.

The Kulango believe in a god who is not worshipped but is addressed in his association with "mother earth." This earth god is the god of the whole tribe. During disasters or hard times, the Kulango pray to the spirits of their ancestors and make offerings to them of mashed yams.

BLENDING RELIGIONS

Over the centuries, both Christian and Islamic rites and beliefs have been incorporated into indigenous religions. New religious movements that contain elements from the different religions have also been formed. Led by individual prophets, these separatist groups mix beliefs from different sources to help people deal with the demands of daily life. Most popular among minority groups resisting domination by stronger groups, such religions are evolving and finding a place among Ivorians. For example, although many of the Anyi have remained Roman Catholic, their neighbors, the Baule, have followed the prophets who promise good fortune to those who adhere to the new dogmas.

Each year, the Ivorian government funds and organizes religious pilgrimages for both Muslims and Christians. This is just one of the ways in which Côte d'Ivoire continues to weave religious tolerance and openness into its foundation. After the March 13, 2016, attack in Grand-Bassam, the president and first lady attended an interfaith ceremony to remember the victims. Present at the ceremony were a Catholic priest, an imam (Islamic leader), and an indigenous priest. Actions like these are not just gestures but important symbols that demonstrate the willingness of the government and the country to respect and accept followers of different religious beliefs.

INTERNET LINKS

https://www.britannica.com/topic/Islam
This online encyclopedia gives an in-depth overview of Islam.

https://www.britannica.com/topic/Yamoussoukro-Basilica
In this article, you can learn more about the Basilica of Our Lady of Peace.

LANGUAGE

68 Km MAN
assè
fognèna
n'orélé
allè
bonjour
anissogoma
ayo
agni'o iya
ougoualo

This street sign welcomes visitors in several different languages common to Côte d'Ivoire.

9

WHEN A COUNTRY GAINS independence and moves on from its colonial heritage, it often adopts new traditions and customs that are entirely different from the former ruling country. Language, however, is often so ingrained in a culture and society that it often stays in place long past independence. A language is kept for convenience on a day-to-day basis, but also because a country's cultural history, including its books and music, are often written in the old language. The national language of Côte d'Ivoire is French, a legacy of the earlier colonial administration.

The name of the country is French, meaning Ivory Coast. Many Ivorians are bilingual, speaking French and their mother tongue, which is the language of their village and ethnic group. With over sixty different ethnic groups, this means that there are as many languages spoken in the country. In fact, by some counts, there are over eighty languages spoken across the nation. Some have been brought by immigrant groups, while others existed within the country long before the colonial period. All indigenous languages represented in Côte d'Ivoire belong to one of four subgroups of the Niger-Congo family: the Kwa in the southeast, the Kru in the southwest, the Mande in the northwest, and the Gur/Senfo in the north and northeast. The official language of the country, however, is French, and it is used in government offices and in all educational institutions.

TONE LANGUAGES

The languages of Côte d'Ivoire are all grouped under the Niger-Congo language family, a group of languages widely spoken in western, northern, and southern Africa. Languages of this family are called tone languages because tones serve phonetically to distinguish the meanings of words. Totally different meanings are distinguished merely by changes in the pitch of a single syllable. These different pitches are crucial to understanding exactly what is said. In such cases, a single word may have a number of different meanings, depending on which syllable is intoned higher or longer or given more stress.

Of the language branches, the Kwa languages have the highest number of speakers today. Kwa is divided into the Baule and Anyi languages, which together are spoken by around three million people. Half of Anyi speakers live in neighboring Ghana. The Mande branch includes the Dan and Guro languages, which can be heard in countries from Sierra Leone to Mali and Guinea-Bissau. Those who speak the Guro language tend to live around the lake region in Côte d'Ivoire. The Kru branch consists of the Kru language spoken by the Kru peoples, whose settlements and language can also be found in Burkina Faso and Liberia. The Gur branch refers to the Senufo language, which is made up of about fifteen unique languages. The Lobi and Kulango languages are among the languages that belong to the Gur branch. Each of these languages also has many dialects. Thus people living in different regions have different pronunciations of the same words. For a characteristic example, the Dyula language has twenty-two dialects.

Dyula, a Mande language, is prominent in Côte d'Ivoire and is also spoken in Burkina Faso and Mali, two of Côte d'Ivoire's close neighbors. It is spoken by millions in West Africa, partially due to the fact that it is a trade language, or a language used for commercial communication among those who might have a variety of different mother tongues that they use at home. Also spelled

Dioula or Jula, this word often denotes people of a specific Mande ethnic group, but it is important to note that the language and the group of people are two different things.

NATIONAL LANGUAGE

French belongs to the Indo-European language family. It is taught in the schools, so anyone who can afford to attend school will be able to speak and write French. Although the language was imposed on Ivorians during colonial days and

Mobile service is becoming faster and more reliable every year.

is not a native language, it provides people with a lingua franca—a common communication tool. Without French, problems would arise when people try to converse in over sixty different languages. It would be impossible to choose any local language as the official one because not more than one-tenth of the population can understand any single native language.

TELLING STORIES

Ivorian cultural expression remains very distinct today, particularly in its oral forms. Although writing traditions exist, Ivorians are primarily a vocal people, as are most Africans. Throughout their history, Ivorians have regarded oral language as a mighty force. All the people share and value this heritage. In a country where many ethnic languages coexist and a colonial language was imposed on everyone, it requires incredible effort to preserve a written literature for each ethnic tongue. Moreover, widespread illiteracy undermines any such concepts. Thus it has been necessary to convey treasuries of African stories, history, and folklore by way of oral traditions.

SHARING INFORMATION

Although freedom of the press is guaranteed in the constitution, in reality it remains restricted. The press consists of many weeklies, dailies, and other

Radio is a popular source of information and entertainment, especially in small villages.

periodicals. During the 2010—2011 civil war, newspapers were used to circulate propaganda from both sides. Almost all publications are in French and are issued in Abidjan. There are nine daily newspapers all told, and four of them are more widely read than the rest—*Fraternité Matin*, owned by the government, *Notre Voie*, *Le Patriote*, and *Soir Info*.

Radio is one of the most popular media in Côte d'Ivoire. Several radio stations exist, broadcasting in French and in the various African languages. There is a tier of low-power, noncommercial community radio stations, including some run by the Catholic Church. One example is Radio Espoir, an Abidjan Catholic station. Radiodiffusion Television Ivoirienne (RTI) is a state-operated radio outlet that runs multiple stations. There are also private stations available in Abidjan and other cities. These include Radio Nostalgie and Radio Jam. La Radio de la Paix is a former UN-run station.

While the independent stations have control over their editorial content, the government exercises considerable pressure over the media to promote government policies. Much of the news is devoted to the activities of the president, the government, and the ruling party. In 1991, a commission was set up to enforce laws against publishing material "undermining the reputation of the nation or defaming institutions of the State." This led to some upsets in the 1990s, and even the jailing of some journalists. Since the end of the 2010—2011 conflict, the media—including state-run outlets—have cut down on inflammatory language.

By 2017, there were 6.3 million internet users in Côte d'Ivoire, or about a quarter of the total population. As of 2017, only about 143,000 residents have fixed broadband subscriptions. The most popular social network is Facebook.

Though Ivorians no longer live under French colonial rule, the history lives on through the French language that is spoken throughout the country. For Ivorians, French unites a diverse people, most of whom also speak one of sixty different mother tongues. When it comes to the Ivorian diaspora living in

There are two popular news sites, Agence Ivoirienne de Presse (AIP), which is owned by the state, and Abidjan.net, a private site.

TELEPHONES TODAY

The Ivorian telephone system is relatively well developed, especially when compared to other African nations. In the late 1990s, the telephone sector changed hands from state-owned to private, and many households began to install fixed lines. In the twenty-first century, cell phones have gained popularity. There are multiple mobile service providers in the market. As of 2017, there were over thirty-one million mobile cellular subscriptions.

Ivorians use their cell phones to talk, text, browse the internet, and play games. Video gaming on cell phones is becoming more popular even though poor reception can be a problem across the country. The number of new fixed internet and broadband connections continues to lag.

neighboring countries and in France, a common language can ease communication and help people feel closer, even when they are physically far away. At this time, there are no major efforts to move away from French as the national language, even though the country has decidedly declared and held tight to its independence for many years.

Today, websites can be translated into a diverse range of languages, from French to indigenous dialects. This article celebrates a social media site being available in a West African language.

INTERNET LINKS

https://www.britannica.com/topic/French-language
Here you can learn more about French, Côte d'Ivoire's official language.

https://www.duolingo.com/course/fr/en/Learn-French-Online
Duolingo offers free courses in French.

https://www.ethnologue.com/country/ci/languages
This site offers a deep dive into Côte d'Ivoire's many languages.

ARTS

From statues and masks to bowls and jewelry, Côte d'Ivoire boasts a wide array of traditional artforms.

10

CÔTE D'IVOIRE IS KNOWN AS AN artistically rich nation with a long history of mask-making, pottery, textiles, and more. For generations, art has served as one expression of unique family and ethnic groups, helping to reinforce and reform religious and social patterns. Whether they are working with wood, fibers, ivory, clay, stone, or metals, Ivorians create functional, beautiful pieces, often in line with traditions that reach back through the centuries. Artists are influenced by a mix of indigenous culture, colonial periods, and even contemporary periods of political and social unrest. As in many countries, art in Côte d'Ivoire is a vehicle for communication and commentary, offering a look into the past while also propelling both artists and viewers into the future.

"It's an asset—a collection of 15,000 pieces from across every region."
—Silvie Memel Kassi, Museum Director, Museum of Civilizations

The civil wars and political unrest of the last few years have affected all aspects of daily life, and museums have not been immune to the destruction. In 2017, Côte d'Ivoire's Museum of Civilizations officially reopened its doors after major looting in 2015 left the museum without many major works and sacred pieces that had been hallmarks of its collection. After the pillaging, which ended with over one hundred pieces stolen, the museum closed for a two-year refurbishment and renovation.

Today, the Museum of Civilizations holds over fifteen thousand objects representing nearly every region in Côte d'Ivoire. It has a conference center, restaurant, and garden. In 2019, the museum plans to open an exhibition on its "ghost collection," highlighting the items that were looted and the issue of illegal art trafficking.

HISTORY

Before Europeans arrived, numerous cultural influences from other parts of Africa had spread through Côte d'Ivoire as a result of the Saharan trade routes. When the French came, they brought their culture and their own artistic traditions with them. Modern Ivorians are greatly influenced by European culture, sometimes to the extent of rejecting indigenous traditions. Fortunately, with the rise in African nationalism, cultural revivals are occurring in all African countries. Côte d'Ivoire is no exception—here, the government encourages and provides support to dance troupes, music groups, artists, writers, and even the museums. Thus, a strong indigenous culture can assert its presence confidently.

The arts of Côte d'Ivoire are distinctive to each ethnic group. For example, a notable Dan carving is that of a large ceremonial spoon for serving rice. These spoons typically have two legs resembling human legs and are known as "Wunkirmian." The Senufo carve ornate doors and drums, often depicting spirits and supernatural beings. The Baule sculpt vessels out of wood and metal to be used for carrying water or practicing divination.

WEARABLE ART

Masks and statues have historically been used, and continue to be used during dances, masquerades, and religious ceremonies. They are usually carved out of single blocks of wood and decorated with clay, shells, beads, ivory, or feathers.

Ivorian art, like much African art, is rooted in ancestor worship. A mask represents the permanent bond between a tribe and its ancestors and is valued for the tradition it represents. The belief is that both people and animals are important parts of the natural order, and that people should experience a oneness with all things in the natural world.

During the construction of an ancestral mask, sculptors carve facial and bodily features differently from those on masks used for entertainment. They adopt communally approved artistic codes, such as the use of white as the color of death or the rendering of animal forms to reinforce the message of the mask. For example, the lion signifies strength, the spider shows prudence, and horns express the moon and fertility.

Today, many masks are on display in the refurbished Museum of Civilizations.

An instrument that is popular in Côte d'Ivoire, but also throughout West Africa, is the shekere. This traditional instrument is made from a dried gourd that is covered with netting that fits close to the instrument's body. Beads or shells are woven into the netting, producing a rustling sound when the gourd is shaken or hit against the hands. The shekere makes a beautiful, rhythmic sound and is often heard in West African and Latin American traditional or folkloric music. Today, you might hear it on a jazz record or used in children's dance music. The shekere is not only an instrument—it also doubles as an art piece. Artists take care to weave colorful beads into intricate patterns on the netting. Constructing a shekere through traditional means can take a long time, as the gourd must first be grown, dried, emptied, scrubbed, and decorated. As an instrument and work of art, the shekere is truly a labor of love.

The most common Dan mask is a human face, slightly abstract but with realistic features, a smooth surface, a pouting mouth, slit or large circular eyeholes, and a calm expression.

Traditionally worn in commemorative ceremonies, Baule facial masks are very realistic and tend to portray living individuals who can be recognized easily by their facial scars or hairstyles.

The masks and figures made by the Senufo people are used in ceremonies organized to honor village life. Senufo masks are highly stylized—the most famous is the "fire spitter" helmet mask, which is a combination of the antelope, warthog, and hyena. Another is the warthog mask, made to exorcise evil spirits. Hornbill figures, in a variety of sizes and styles, are important because that bird was the mythological founder of the Senufo people and a symbol of fertility. Dance masks are used in village masquerades at the end of harvest festivities.

Though Ivorians have always been committed to making brilliant art, much of the nation's oldest pieces of pottery, jewelry, masks, and other artifacts no longer reside in the country in which they were created. During the colonial period, artistic objects, many of them owned by indigenous peoples, were removed to France, where they now reside in museums. Over the years, many African nations have called for the return of their art and artifacts, as they are an important part of each country's own history. However, museums have long been resistant to the idea of handing over these valuable, delicate pieces. In late 2018, French experts released a report recommending that the French federal government create a new law that would legislate the return of art to countries that request it. Currently, French law forbids the country from ceding objects owned by the state, and the proposed changes, if they go into effect, would be a long-awaited step forward.

MUSIC AND DANCE

Ivorian traditions have unified the masquerade, music, and dance as the symbolic continuation of creation and life. The musician's role is to invoke the spirit to enter the masquerader, after which the mask and dancer are considered sacred and not to be desecrated. During the masquerade, the masked dancer is granted a symbolic status, and any utterances that the dancer makes are believed to be coming from the ancestor or god that is now in possession of his or her body. In such a ritual, the supernatural often becomes an actual presence, ready to intervene in the affairs of the living.

The resonating space inside a completed instrument is believed to give fullness to the ancestral voices, and it is the musician's performance on particular instruments that enables the ancestors to reveal themselves through the moving bodies of the dancers.

A dancer's body is thus considered an instrument that can be played by a skilled musician. The dancer, who is knowledgeable in the language of the

One genre that is popular with the youngest generations of Ivorians is "Coupé-Décalé." Advanced by DJs in both France and Côte d'Ivoire, the dance sounds are percussive, featuring African samples and heavy bass. While the genre was created by the Ivorian diaspora living in Paris and DJ-ing at African clubs, some say it helped unite the politically divided country during times of strife. The lyrics tend to deal with money, relationships, staying positive, and "making it" abroad.

Some of the most well-known Coupé-Décalé artists include Meiway, DJ Arafat, DJ Allan, DJ Lewis, Bloco, and Papa Fololo. There have been several "waves" of the genre, beginning around 2002 and extending into the present day. Each wave has been led by new artists, fresh dance moves, and new perspectives on the music.

music, makes certain audible or physical responses to particular sounds and rhythms, thereby translating these sounds into a dialogue with the ancestor.

MUSICAL TRADITIONS

Drum ensembles consisting of three to five musicians who play connecting patterns are common in Côte d'Ivoire.

The country's traditional music is characterized by a series of melodies and rhythms occurring in harmony. It may seem monotonous to some people, but in fact, African rhythms have influenced Western popular music such as jazz, blues, and even rock.

Music is used to transmit knowledge and values and for celebrating communal and personal events. Stages of a person's life are marked with music specific to adolescent initiation rites, weddings, ancestral ceremonies, and funerals.

Traditional music involves the use of a large assortment of instruments that are made with local materials. Drums are among the most popular instruments used. They come in a number of shapes, such as cylindrical, kettle, and hourglass. Several materials, such as wood, gourds, and clay, are used to construct drum bodies. Membranes are made from the skins of reptiles, cattle, goats, and other animals. The beautiful drums provide many different musical voices.

Other important percussion instruments include clap sticks, bells, rattles, gourds, clay pots, and xylophones. Stringed instruments include the musical bow, lute, and harp. The flute, whistle, oboe, and trumpet are the wind instruments. Flutes are made from bamboo, reeds, wood, clay, or bones. Trumpets are made from corn stems from the savanna areas with a reed sliced from the surface of the stem at one end.

Historically, traditional music and spoken word have been the prerogative of one esteemed social group, the griots. They played a crucial role as historians in the kingdoms that developed from the tenth century to the twentieth century across Africa as a whole and in Côte d'Ivoire in particular. They advised courts, told stories, and led praise songs. They were drawn from five griot families and were eventually considered a social caste all their own. This caste remains dedicated to preserving the memories of society through words and music, and the griot's work is still practiced today, usually for a fee. The work is considered a service and is often performed for nobility, formal ceremonies, baptisms, weddings, and funerals. Today's griots can be male or female, and they often play percussion instruments as well as lutes.

Many types of music, including jazz music, performed here by Manu Dibango, are popular in Côte d'Ivoire.

CONTEMPORARY MUSIC

Ivorian popular music is an amazing blend of African, European, American, and Middle Eastern traditions. It evolved from musicians and others who came to this country during the twentieth century. Ballads were introduced during that time, and sailors from all over the world exposed the Ivorians to accordions and stringed instruments such as guitars. The subsequent development of popular music has been powerfully influenced by electronic mass media and the growing popularity of African music in the international music scene of the late twentieth and early twenty-first centuries.

Today, young Ivorians enjoy Jamaican reggae, Caribbean "zouk" music, and hip-hop styles imported from the United States. Abidjan is home to live musical performances from local artists as well as international musicians. Since 2005, it has been home to a hip-hop contest called Faya Flow.

INDIGENOUS DANCE

Dance is as varied in style and function as music. Dancing is associated with both sacred and secular events, and it plays a crucial role in education, work, entertainment, politics, and religious ritual. Common dance patterns include team dances using formations; group dances that invite individuals to showcase their skills; and solo dances, often performed by a professional entertainer.

Dancers of a group called Jouvay Fest perform during an arts festival in Abidjan in March 2018.

In 2017, a new literary activist movement started cropping up on the social media site Twitter. #AbidjanLit began sparking conversations and meet-ups about language, books, literature, and so much more. Those involved in the #AbidjanLit movement seek to explore what it means to be a reader and a writer in West Africa. As a nation with a long colonial history, Côte d'Ivoire is home to a wide variety of languages and cultures, which means that the literary scene is similarly diverse. With #AbidjanLit, readers and writers are better able to discuss that diversity and recognize it as a strength and gift that they, as residents of Côte d'Ivoire, are lucky to access.

Body postures in Ivorian dance are typically earth-oriented movements in which the performer bends the knees and inclines the torso forward from the hips.

One of the most well-known dances is the Zouli, a form of dance and music practiced by the Guro communities. Zouli is an homage to feminine beauty and weaves together masks, costumes, instruments, song, and dance. There are seven different masks worn during the dance, each with its own legend. Another longstanding dance is called N'Goron. This dance, derived from the Senufo people, involves an elaborate costume of feathers, grass skirts, shells, and a hat made from sheep skin. It is an initiation dance meant for young Senufo girls.

This *korhogo* cloth was woven and painted by Senufo villagers in northern Côte d'Ivoire.

CLOTH

The Ivorians consider textiles and the decorative arts used in textiles as works of art and as significant social communication between family members. In particular, the art of making *korhogo* cloth is a tradition that is handed down from one generation to another. *Korhogo* cloth is a fabric woven by Senufo weavers that is then hand painted. The intricate symbols and patterns skillfully drawn on the cloth are evidence of their mastery of the traditional art of making textiles. The cloth is recognizable by the bold figures, usually dark brown or black, painted on plain cotton material, usually white.

Korhogo artists cooperate in an organized manner. The cotton spinning and dyeing are done by women, and the weaving is handled by men. The dye used for hand painting on the cloth is a mixture extracted from the bark and leaves of a shrub. It is used to draw mostly geometric figures and animal motifs such as chickens, lizards, and snakes. Traditionally, the decorated material was used by young people being initiated and by hunters and dancers.

WRITERS

Over the years, Côte d'Ivoire has nurtured a diverse group of Ivorian writers. From poets and novelists to journalists and playwrights, many beautiful words have sprung from the coast of West Africa. Arguably, Côte d'Ivoire's most famous and prolific writer is Bernard Dadié, whose work has been widely translated. One of his novels, *An African in Paris*, published in 1959, is an autobiographical account of a childhood journey to France. Other translated works are *The Black Cloth* and *The City Where No One Dies*. Other well-known

Serge Bilé, a French-Ivorian writer, poses at the library of the French Cultural Center in Abidjan in 2018.

national novelists include Aké Loba and Ahmadou Kourouma. Loba was best known for *Kocoumbo*, an autobiographical novel of a young African suffering the effects of being uprooted and poverty-stricken in Paris who is drawn toward militant communism. Kourouma's best-selling novel, *The Suns of Independence*, tells the story of a village chief deposed after independence, losing his subjects, and having to adjust to a different life. The national library is located in Abidjan. Constructed in the 1970s, the building itself was a gift from Canada, though most of the building has been closed since 2006 due to lack of funding. The juvenile section remains open.

Côte d'Ivoire's rich history of the arts reaches past its colonial period and into ancient indigenous cultures. Today, it is the challenge of contemporary artists and supporters of the arts to marry all of the time periods together to tell the complete story of Côte d'Ivoire. This is being done through dance, sculpture, textiles, literature, and so much more. As the country continues to recover from the looting and devastation of recent wars and unrest, it has the opportunity to reinvest in museums, arts education, and other methods for centering art in the nation once again.

INTERNET LINKS

https://www.abidjan.com/v/exhibitions
At this website, check out popular museums and exhibitions in Côte d'Ivoire.

https://www.empiretextiles.com/blog
This blog features articles all about West African fashion trends and traditions.

http://www.nationallibraryofcotedivoire.org
The National Library of Côte d'Ivoire has its own website where you can explore its history and current activities.

https://twitter.com/AbidjanLit
This website is the home of the Abidjan Lit Collective.

LEISURE

Football (soccer) is an extremely
popular sport in Côte d'Ivoire.

JUST LIKE ANY OTHER COUNTRY, Côte d'Ivoire is home to a healthy mix of work and leisure. Ivorians work hard, but they enjoy activities and communal celebrations during their "off" time. Holidays and festivals are always times of cheer, but games, sports, arts, dancing, and other activities are enjoyed all year long. On weekends, those who live in cities like to escape to Grand-Bassam, a coastal town with colonial history, charming buildings, and sandy beaches. Additionally, whether they are participating or watching, Ivorians enjoy sports and games. From national teams to backyard games, competition is fun and fierce.

GAMES

Similar to backgammon, the game of *awale* (a-WA-lay) is an intellectual pastime enjoyed by Ivorians of all ages. It can be played by two people or by teams of more people. The rules are not difficult, but playing the

Storytelling is a common practice in Côte d'Ivoire, just as it is across the globe. Here, this teacher tells her students a story.

game well takes a lot of practice. The *awale* board is rectangular and about 20 inches (51 cm) long, with two rows of six cups each. Game pieces are forty-eight peas or pebbles. There are several versions of the game, a variant of mancala, played by the different ethnic groups, but certain features are common in all versions.

To start the game, four peas are placed in each cup. The first player starts by picking up all the peas from any cup on his or her side of the board and dropping them one at a time in each consecutive cup to the right, counterclockwise. A person scores by capturing peas, and the winner is the one who captures the most peas. A person captures peas only when the last pea dropped falls in a cup on the opponent's side that contains only one or two peas. When that happens, the player picks up all the peas in that cup and sets them aside for counting at the end of the game.

STORIES

Stories help people perceive who they are in relation to others and often aid in the understanding of a culture. Ivorian storytelling is full of wisdom, experience, and the teachings of a people who depended on an oral tradition to pass stories, legends, and histories from one generation to another. These beloved accounts are powerful educational tools because they can teach the listeners some important lessons about traditional community life and values. Accompanied by music and sometimes dance, the stories can be about people, animals, or spirits, whether they are good or evil. The stories introduce their hearers to a world of knowledge, mystery, and magic that appeals to their emotions. Children love to listen to the stories their elders tell them. They often gather in a communal area for some enthralling stories when the elders are free to tell them.

ATHLETICS

Rugby is a popular sport in Côte d'Ivoire. There is a national team, and though relatively inexperienced, the members participate in the World Cup

Just as it has swept the rest of the world, video gaming has become a popular pastime in Côte d'Ivoire in recent years. Each year, millions of West Africans play video games on consoles and smartphones, and the industry itself is looking to locate new jobs on the continent. In 2017, Abidjan hosted Africa's largest video game festival, the Electronic and Video Game Festival of Abidjan, or FEJA. It welcomed tens of thousands of video game enthusiasts and investors. Visitors to FEJA discussed opportunities for the video gaming industry in Côte d'Ivoire, but they also noted setbacks such as slow internet connections, a lack of technology education, and expensive internet and data plans.

championship games. Basketball and softball are also widely played. Golf can be played as Abidjan and Yamoussoukro each have good courses with grass greens. Because golf is such an expensive sport, the good courses are used mostly by tourists or businessmen. Locals are more likely to be seen on a less desirable course made of sand and artificial fibers. Surfing, for those who can afford the expensive equipment, is available at the beaches. Most people opt to swim in pools found at the big hotels and in some of the main cities, as strong currents along the coast make swimming there dangerous.

During a friendly match in 2018, Max-Alain Gradel of Côte d'Ivoire (*right*) kicks the ball in front of a player from Togo (*left*).

Soccer is by far the nation's favorite sport. People there call it football. There are matches to watch every Sunday in the major cities. Unofficial games are always being played on the beach, in the streets, or at the university or municipal stadium. From an early age, boys are encouraged to take up the sport. The Ivorians are proud of their national soccer team. The national team is controlled by the Fédération Ivoirienne de Football. There are also a number of Ivorian soccer players who play in internationally renowned soccer clubs.

One such player is Eric Bailly, who plays for Manchester United, an English Premier League club.

HAVING FUN

Côte d'Ivoire is home to many national parks, making exploration and hiking favorite pastimes of locals, as well as tourists. Water sports such as surfing and sailing are popular in Abidjan.

With adults, dancing is very popular. Dance clubs are the favorite entertainment spots for younger people. On weekends, these lively clubs become very crowded. Movie theaters attract large audiences, too, with three to four showings a day in big cities such as Yamoussoukro and Bouaké. Most city residents can afford this cheap but enjoyable diversion.

Côte d'Ivoire is a nation of young people. With a high percentage of its population under the age of fifteen, the country will be forced, in coming years, to provide more entertainment options for teens and young adults. Today,

Ivorians love to watch their national football team, especially when it is time for the FIFA World Cup.

FANTASTIC FOOTBALL

Just as it is in many African countries and throughout Europe, soccer is a major sport in Côte d'Ivoire. A soccer field will be found in almost every town and village, and there is at least one soccer club in every city. Some famous Ivorian soccer players include Didier Drogba, Salomon Kalou, and Emmanuel Eboué. The national team qualified for all three FIFA World Cups held between 2006 and 2015, though it never advanced beyond the group stage. However, the national team continues to have a large following and has had many notable wins in other international matches, including the championship title at the 2015 Africa Cup of Nations. It is widely considered to be one of the best teams on the continent. Their nickname, the Elephants, is reflected in the elephant on their logo.

sports remain extremely popular, especially as FIFA becomes more well known and more opportunities arise for children to play soccer competitively. The twenty-first century has brought video gaming and other digital hobbies into focus, and we can expect to see that trend continue. For Ivorians, leisure time looks different depending on your age, home region, income level, and other factors. Luckily, there are a range of options available for every individual and family who needs a little time to rest and relax.

INTERNET LINKS

https://www.fifa.com/worldcup/teams/team=43854/groups.html
Here, you can see the FIFA homepage for Côte d'Ivoire's national soccer team.

https://www.ictj.org/news/cote-divoire-youth-political-voice -stories-war
This article details the power of storytelling for youth in a postwar Côte d'Ivoire.

https://sofitel.accorhotels.com/gb/hotel-8844-sofitel-abidjan -hotel-ivoire/index.shtml
This is the website of the grand Hotel Ivoire in Abidjan.

FESTIVALS

One of the largest and most popular festivals in Côte d'Ivoire involves costumes, dancing, and of course—masks.

CÔTE D'IVOIRE, THANKS TO ITS variety of religions and tribes, as well as its long and storied history, is a place of cultural and artistic abundance. There is no better way to experience this than to take in a festival or holiday with Ivorians. While many are closely tied to religious beliefs and practices, others are secular in nature. Ritual celebrations, initiation ceremonies, and coming-of-age ceremonies are all part of a full annual calendar of events.

12

In one Ramadan tradition, a sacrificed animal is divided into three portions: the first one for the family, the second for relatives and friends, and the third share for the poor and needy.

CHRISTIAN CELEBRATIONS

Christian Ivorians, many of whom are Evangelical, Catholic, or Methodist, celebrate several holidays throughout the year. Easter, which celebrates the resurrection of Jesus Christ, is usually in April. Ascension Day, marking the rising of Christ into heaven on the fortieth day after the resurrection, is celebrated in May. Whitsunday falls on the seventh Sunday after Easter. This festival commemorates the descent of the Holy Spirit on the day of Pentecost. Assumption Day, the reception of the Virgin Mary into heaven, is in August. All Saints' Day on November 1 honors loved ones who have died. Christmas Day celebrates the birth of Jesus Christ.

ISLAMIC HOLY DAYS

Men join together over soup in order to break their fast during Ramadan, a Muslim holy month.

A large portion of Ivorians are Muslims, or followers of Islam.

Muslims observe Ramadan, which is the ninth month of the Islamic lunar calendar. During the month of Ramadan, Muslims fast between sunrise and sunset. According to the fourth pillar of Islam, fasting brings one closer to Allah, or God. The discipline of fasting reminds Muslims of people who are deprived of life's basic necessities and the sufferings of less fortunate people. It also encourages Muslims to show compassion and kindness toward people in need. The festival begins with a special prayer performed in a mosque. After the prayer, people greet each other warmly and give presents to the children. Then they visit relatives and friends, and everyone asks for forgiveness for any wrongdoings in the previous year.

Ramadan ends with a huge feast, called the Feast of Breaking the Fast, or Eid al-Fitr, which follows the sighting of the new moon. It is a joyous occasion when everyone prays together, visits friends and relatives, exchanges gifts, and eats lots of very good food. In many ways, it is similar to the spirit of the American Thanksgiving. On Eid al-Fitr, Muslims express thanks for health, strength, and the opportunities in life given to them by Allah. Although the celebration lasts for two to ten days, depending on the region, the main activities occur on the first day, the new moon.

OTHER TRADITIONS

THE FEAST OF DIPRI, or Fête du Dipri, takes place in April in Gomon, 62 miles (100 km) northwest of Abidjan. This is the home of the Abidji, the local ethnic group. It celebrates local folklore surrounding initiation and coming-of-age. The entire village stays awake all night within the safety of their huts. Around midnight, women and children sneak out of their huts to carry out nocturnal

THE MASK FESTIVAL

The Festival of Masks, or Fête des Masques, is one of the most popular festivals of the region. It is celebrated in November in the city of Man, and during this time many small villages hold competitions to select the best mask dancer, while prudently paying homage to the forest spirits who are personified in these masks. Two famous dances are the stilt dance and the jugglers' dance.

Masked dancers ask the spirits for blessings, for help, and for protection from future harm. During times of political unrest and upheaval, the Festival of Masks was seen by some as a unifying tool. During the celebration, people from all over the country join together over three days, not only to celebrate their heritage but to look toward a positive future.

rites to cleanse the village of evil spells. Before sunrise, the chief appears, calling out to his people, "Chase out the evil."

Then, drums play and people go into frenzied trances. The goals of the festival are to drive out evil spirits, purify villagers, and resolve conflicts.

YAM FESTIVALS are celebrated at the beginning and end of harvests with music, dances, and masquerades. The yam is such an integral part of the people's diet that a good harvest makes a great difference in their lives. The Ivorians take this opportunity, therefore, to honor the ancestors and spirits who protect their crops and to invite their good graces.

For the Anyi and Baule people, the yam festival starts with the *anaya* (a-NAI-ya), a food offering to the gods, on the third Friday in October. After the *anaya*, festivities are stopped for one month. At that time, a memorial service is conducted for those who have died, and a purification rite is enacted to rid the village of evil influences. During the celebration, a purification bundle, which

These women sing and talk as they grind yams during the yam festival.

includes a shoot of oil palm tree, a bush rope, and branches of the *atiz-dize* tree, is prepared. In the evening, the bundle is carried aloft in a procession and then buried with prayers that no evil will cross the site. Farmers then carry in the new yam crop, and everyone tastes the fruits of the harvest.

For the Abron people, the yam festival is also a time to commemorate their arrival in Côte d'Ivoire from the east. The event is lavish, with the enthroned king presiding over the festivities. He is dressed in a richly embroidered toga, wears a gold tiara, and holds in his right hand a solid gold scepter. He is covered by a huge scarlet canopy. All around him are his subjects in bright costumes, sitting under colorful umbrellas.

To observe the yam festival, Kulango parents and children exchange gifts and eat a meal of mashed yams and soup. Dances and singing are part of the celebrations. For some clans, crops other than yams may be just as important. For example, the Dan people rely heavily on rice as a staple. If a rice harvest is good, young Dan girls will perform a dance of homage to the spirits protecting the crops.

CELEBRATING CHRISTMAS

In North America, there are certain traditions surrounding Christmas Eve and Christmas Day that we expect to see each year. The same can be said of those living in Côte d'Ivoire, though the traditions there look a little different from those in the West. Ivorians celebrate Christmas with church services that last all night long, from the evening of December 24 through 6 a.m. on December 25. There are active worship sessions that include singing, group dancing, poems, skits, testimonies, and more. A minister gives a sermon, and prayers are offered.

When it comes to exchanging gifts, Ivorians wait until the new year, bypassing any gift-giving on Christmas morning. Gifts in the new year signal good prosperity and hope in the year to come.

Across the country, inside mosques and churches, in the village centers, and on city streets, Ivorians have always celebrated their traditional festivals and holidays with energy and excitement. Traditions have held strong. As a developing country, Côte d'Ivoire's holidays are marked by time spent with others, religious rituals, and folkloric crafts rather than the shopping-related traditions of North America. Time will tell whether local traditions will stay in place or be subsumed by corporate interests as the country continues to grow as an economic power.

INTERNET LINKS

https://publicholidays.africa/ivory-coast
This website includes updated dates for holidays celebrated in Côte d'Ivoire.

http://www.transafrica.biz/festivals/festivals-events-ivory-coast
Take a deeper dive into traditional festivals and dances in the country at this website.

FOOD

Cassava, a root vegetable, is also known as "manioc."
Here, it has been peeled and is being cleaned.

13

LIKE ALL COUNTRIES, CÔTE D'IVOIRE features a wide variety of food options throughout the country's many cities and regions. Some harken back to indigenous and colonial traditions, while others are more contemporary. The over sixty ethnic groups that call the country home add a high level of diversity to the cuisine, though grains and tubers remain the bedrocks of the diet.

Cassava is a tropical perennial plant introduced in Côte d'Ivoire by Portuguese sailors returning from Brazil in the sixteenth century.

MEALTIME

In the Ivorian society, eating is not simply a matter of sustaining the body but an expression of the community spirit. In rural areas and villages, the tradition is for all the people in a village to eat together in a common area. The villagers are divided into three groups—women and girls eat as one group, men as another, and young boys as the third. Food is served in large containers and placed on mats on the ground. There is no need for utensils, as the Ivorians use their clean right hands to scoop up food instead of knives and forks. Usually a handful of rice is taken and formed into a ball along with some meat and sauce. After the meal, a washbasin is passed around.

IVORIAN SPECIALTIES

Chicken and fish are the favorite foods of Ivorians, but vegetables make up a large part of an Ivorian's diet and provide for significant amounts of vitamins. A typical meal includes a staple, such as rice or cassava, and a sauce in which to dip the rice. Leafy vegetables, root crops, and hot peppers are commonly boiled or added to soups and stews. Ivorians typically do not eat a dessert, but sometimes fresh fruit is served after a meal.

HOT PEPPERS originated in South America. Today they are a staple in Côte d'Ivoire, where several varieties are cultivated for local use. There are many kinds of hot peppers of interesting colors and shapes and with varying degrees of hotness. Habanero, a type of hot pepper, is more widely cultivated than any other variety and is one of the hottest. The fruit of the habanero has a smoky flavor and is usually red or yellow. Ivorians use habanero to spice up virtually every dish on the table because its smoky aroma adds a familiar special taste to soups, stews, and sauces.

Yams, a popular staple on Ivorian tables, are sold in a Bouaké market.

Outdoor markets are a favorite of tourists and residents alike. Here, street vendors serve food cooked over a low fire, such as chicken, fish, onions, rice, and tomatoes. These open-air restaurants are also known as "maquis," and they are unique to Côte d'Ivoire. Vendors braise food over a fire, and then it is sold to passersby, usually for a reasonable price. Some markets also sell attiéké, *a side dish made of cassava, or* kedjenou, *a slow-cooked stew. The sight and smell of* kedjenou *in its sealed pot, cooking over the coals, is enough to make anyone's mouth water.*

YAMS are widely cultivated in Côte d'Ivoire. Both the leaves and the root are eaten. The leaves are steamed and cooked in palm oil with okra, lima beans, hot peppers, and smoked fish, and usually served with rice. The roots may be peeled and boiled or used to make french fries. Yams can range in color from yellow to orange-red to purple, and can be classified into two types—dry or moist. Dry yams have a powdery texture after cooking. Yams are often added to onions and tomatoes and sautéed with peppers. The mixture is boiled until the yams are soft.

OKRA is another widely grown plant. A typical okra can grow up to 6 feet (1.8 m) tall. The leaves are lobed and are generally hairy. The plant first produces dark yellow flowers and then pods, which are the edible portions of the plant. Young pods are thinly sliced to prepare okra soup. Tough and fibrous pods are dried and then ground into a powder, which is used for thickening stews. Fresh young pods can be dried for use anytime in soups.

CASSAVA, also known as tapioca, is divided into sweet and bitter types. Ivorians enjoy cassava as a daily staple, like rice, because it is nutritious and grows easily under a variety of conditions. Both the roots and leaves are edible. Cooking cassava can be an arduous task because the root contains cyanide, a potentially poisonous salt. Only after grating, squeezing out the liquid, and cooking is cassava safe to eat.

In Côte d'Ivoire, there are many popular dishes people enjoy making and eating. These are just some of them.

ALOCO *(AL-oh-ko) is ripe bananas cooked in palm oil and garnished with steamed onions and chilies. It can be eaten alone or with grilled fish.*

ATTIÉKÉ *(AT-tee-eck-eh) is a popular side dish of grated cassava. Attiéké is like couscous, which is a dish of prepared wheat pellets steamed over broth with meat or fruit added, prevalent in many parts of Africa. In Côte d'Ivoire, it is made with cassava.*

KEDJENOU *(KED-gen-ooh) is chicken cooked with different kinds of vegetables in a mild sauce. It is cooked in a clay pot over a low fire or wrapped in banana leaves and buried in hot wood ashes. This dish can be served with yams,* attiéké, *or rice.*

FUFU *(FOO-fue) is mashed bananas, typically possessing a sweet flavor.*

FOUTOU *(FOO-too) is made by boiling cassava and bananas until cooked. The cassava and banana are then separately pounded, with drops of water added from time to time to avoid sticking and to bring them to the desired consistency. Then they are mixed together and pounded again, with a little salt added for taste. Unlike* fufu, foutou *is not a sweet dish.*

EGGPLANT has erect or spreading branches bearing egg-shaped white or beautiful dark purple fruit. It is cooked in the same way as other vegetables.

DRINKS

Ivorians enjoy drinking ginger beer, a soft drink made with a lot of ginger, almost enough to burn the throat. To make ginger beer, about 1 pound of peeled and mashed gingerroot and an unpeeled pineapple are added to about 2 quarts (1.89 liters) of boiling water. Lime juice, raisins, or guava may also be used. The mixture is left to stand overnight. The next day, it is strained to remove the fruit, sugar is added, and the drink is chilled.

One of the most popular and unique foods enjoyed by Ivorians is the giant land snail. These massive creatures are considered a delicacy and are so large that some shells can be as big as a human hand. While escargot (snails) are popular in France, their size is small compared to Ivorian snails. The snails, which can be rubbery, are usually served cooked in savory sauces.

As the snails have gained popularity and become favorites of tourists and ex-pats, or people who have left their country to live abroad, the land snails have begun to make their way to the United States. There they are considered an invasive species, since they can contain parasitic, meningitis-causing worms. They have become a serious issue in parts of southern Florida, where they are now plentiful.

Not many Ivorians drink beer, except those living along the coast. There is a good local brew called Flag. A homemade drink is *bangui* (BAN-kee), a local white palm wine. Yeast is added to the juice tapped from a palm tree, and the mixture is left to ferment overnight. Soft drinks are the most popular beverages among women and youths.

RESTAURANTS

The cities have many restaurants, and Abidjan in particular has eating places serving a variety of ethnic foods—French, Italian, Caribbean, Lebanese, and Vietnamese. There are a growing number of establishments catering to non-Africans who want to sample traditional local food. Among them, the maquis eateries are the most popular. They are inexpensive outdoor cafés with chairs and tables or wooden benches and sometimes a sandy floor, and are found almost everywhere throughout the country. Popular dishes in a maquis include braised chicken or fish with onions and tomatoes, *attiéké*, and *kedjenou*. To be considered a maquis, braised food—slow cooked with a little moisture—must be available. A maquis usually opens only in the evenings.

At lunchtime in the cities, waitresses set up stands outside established restaurants to serve rice or *foutou* with various sauces. Patrons make their choices from delicacies such as fish sauce or gumbo sauce, and then go inside to eat. This service is especially useful for the busy urbanites who drop by for a quick, tasty lunch.

BUYING FOOD

Food is more than just a base necessity in Côte d'Ivoire. It incorporates a lifestyle that defines community spirit. Unfortunately, the world was severely impacted by a food price crisis from 2007 to 2008. Those two years saw a dizzying increase in food prices, igniting a global emergency and bringing on political and economic instability and social unrest in poor and undeveloped nations. There are several factors said to have caused the crisis, such as bad weather resulting in poor yields; the heightened cost of fertilizers, food transportation, and industrial agriculture; and growing consumer demand across the expanding middle-class populations in Asia. Some observers have even said that the food crisis stemmed from unprecedented global population growth. This led to the universal challenge of producing enough food for the ever-expanding population in the shortest amount of time and with the world's limited resources.

Some of the worst instability resulting from high food costs was felt in West Africa. One person was killed and dozens were injured as riots tore through Côte d'Ivoire after the prices of meat and wheat increased by 50 percent within a week. President Laurent Gbagbo was forced to cut taxes to deal with the turbulence. Violent protests also broke out in Cameroon, Burkina Faso, and Senegal.

Luckily, the global community acted together to find resolutions to the tough situation. The UN created a high-level task force to bolster cooperation, particularly between developing nations.

Today, food prices in Côte d'Ivoire are no longer at crisis levels. Though the cost of living remains high, the natural resources available within the country, as well as its location on the coast, mean that most families are able to acquire enough food to sustain themselves. More so than some other countries in sub-Saharan Africa, Côte d'Ivoire has a more developed grocery retail market. There are many independent retailers, but French supermarket chains have become interested in expanding to the country too. Additionally, cities continue to see the opening of restaurants, including those that cook traditional Ivorian food and others that offer international cuisines. In 2015, the country received its first Burger King franchise. While more changes are on the horizon, rural areas continue to stick to traditional foods and preparations, and residents retain a rich culture of sharing meals with families, friends, and visitors.

Supermarkets in Abidjan are similar to others around the world.

INTERNET LINKS

https://www.nielsen.com/ssa/en/press-room/2017/supermarket-surge-on-the-cards-for-ivory-coast.html
More insight into the world of Côte d'Ivoire's supermarkets can be found here.

https://safarijunkie.com/ivory-coast/5-must-eat-dishes-in-ivory-coast
This site offers five must-eat dishes from Côte d'Ivoire.

KEDJENOU CHICKEN

1 whole chicken, 4 to 5 pounds, skin on,
    cut into medium pieces
2 medium onions
2 green onion
1 fresh red or green pepper
4 tomatoes
1 tablespoon ginger paste
1 tablespoon garlic puree
1 sprig fresh thyme
1 bay leaf
1 teaspoon smoked paprika
½ tablespoon chicken bouillon, or more
    (optional)
1 whole habanero pepper (optional)
Salt and pepper to taste

Trim chicken of excess fat, pat dry with a cloth or paper napkin, and place in a large pot.

Season chicken with salt, garlic, ginger, thyme, paprika, green onions, chicken bouillon, and onions. Lit sit at least 2 hours or preferably overnight in the fridge for optimal flavor.

Preheat oven to 350°F.

Slice tomatoes, onion, green onions, and red or green pepper.

Combine all the ingredients and stir until everything is fully combined.

Cover the pot with its lid.

Place pot in the oven and shake it once or twice during cooking, without opening the pot.

Bake for about 1 hour until chicken is tender.

Serve with *attiéké* or white rice.

BAKED YAMS

Yams are a popular dish during Eid al-Fitr, the feast that ends the fast during the month of Ramadan. About 43 percent of Ivorians are affiliated with Islam, so the feast is a popular practice throughout much of the country.

5 cups yam pieces, boiled
1 egg, beaten
1 egg yolk, beaten
1 tablespoon room-temperature butter
Salt
Nutmeg
Cinnamon

Boil the yam pieces until soft. Then mash the pieces in a mixing bowl using a spoon or a mixer.

Add the beaten egg, butter, and salt slowly. Mix well until all ingredients are blended.

Spoon the mixture into an oven-safe casserole dish. Spread the beaten egg yolk on top.

Bake for 15 minutes or until golden brown. Sprinkle with nutmeg and cinnamon when done.

Serve hot.

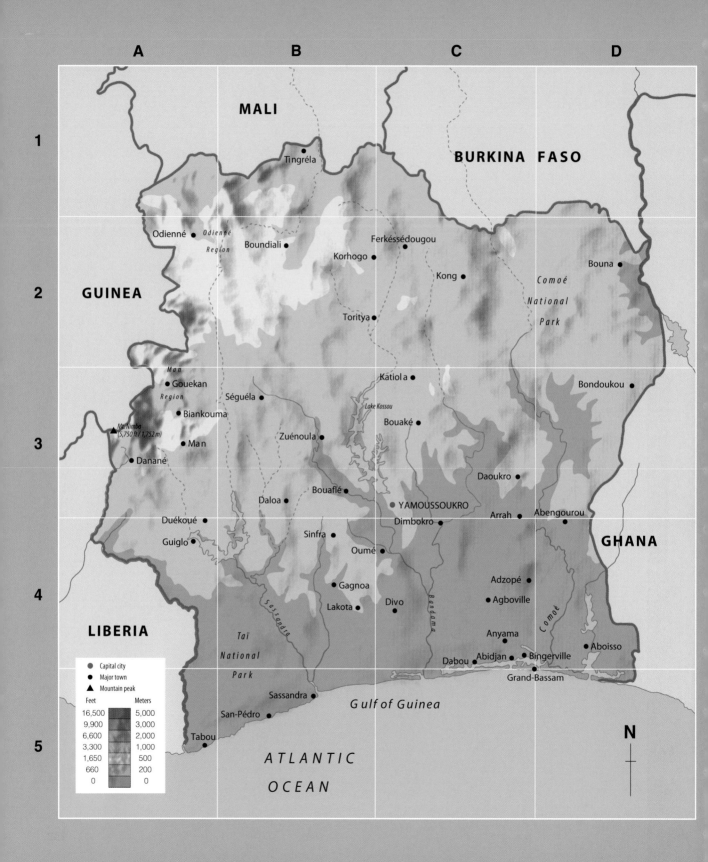

MAP OF CÔTE D'IVOIRE

Abengourou, D4
Abidjan, C4
Aboisso, D4
Adzopé, C4
Agboville, C4
Anyama, C4
Arrah, C3
Atlantic Ocean, A5, B5, C5, D5

Bandama River, C4
Biankouma, A3
Bingerville, C4
Bondoukou, D3
Bouaflé, B3
Bouaké, C3
Bouna, D2
Boundiali, B2
Burkina Faso, C1, D1

Comoé National Park, C2, D2
Comoé River, C2—C3, D3—D4

Dabou, C4
Daloa, B3
Danané, A3
Daoukro, C3
Dimbokro, C4

Divo, C4
Duékoué, A4

Ferkéssédougou, C2

Gagnoa, B4
Ghana, D1—D5
Gouekan, A3
Grand-Bassam, C4
Guiglo, A4
Guinea, A1—A3
Gulf of Guinea, B5, C5, D5

Katiola, C3
Kong, C2
Korhogo, B2

Lake Kossou, B3, C3
Lakota, B4
Liberia, A3—A5

Mali, A1, B1, C1
Man, A3
Man Region, A3
Mt. Nimba, A3

Odienné, A2
Odienné Region, A2, B2
Oumé, C4

San-Pédro, B5
Sassandra, B5
Sassandra River, B4—B5
Séguéla, B3
Sinfra, B4

Tabou, A5
Taï National Park, B4—B5
Tingréla, B1
Tortiya, B2

Yamoussoukro, C3

Zuénoula, B3

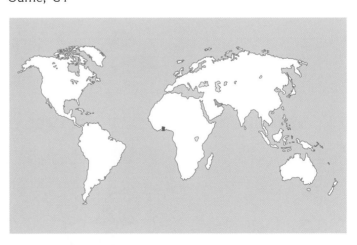

ECONOMIC CÔTE D'IVOIRE

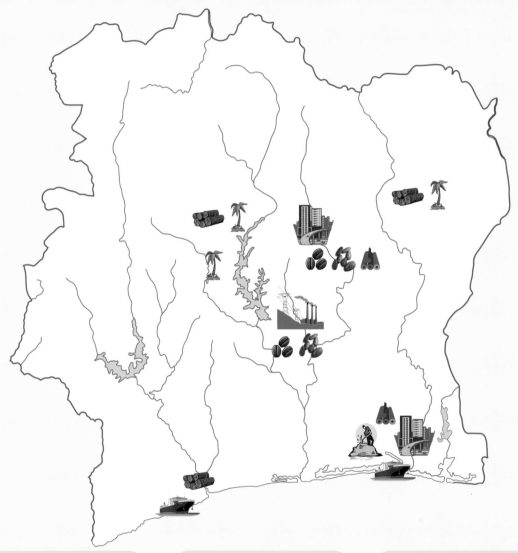

Agriculture

 Cocoa

Coffee

Manufacturing

 Textiles

Services

 Cultural
& political center

 Power plant

 Ports

Natural Resources

 Mines

 Palm oil

 Timber

OVERVIEW

Agriculture is one of Côte d'Ivoire's main economic sectors and is responsible for about two-thirds of employment. The export of agricultural products, such as cocoa, coffee, and palm oil, has also made the country one of the most economically successful among West African nations. The government has been seeking to diversify the economy and is looking into oil exploration and oil and gas production. The country's economic potential and growth have been undermined by civil unrest and political instability, but conditions have been improving over the last eight years, and the economy has begun to improve.

GROSS DOMESTIC PRODUCT (GDP)

$97.16 billion (2017 estimate)

ANNUAL GDP GROWTH

7.8 percent (2017 estimate)

GDP PER CAPITA

$3,900 (2017 estimate)

CURRENCY

West African CFA franc
US$1 = 581 West African CFA francs
(January 2019)

STRUCTURE OF THE ECONOMY AS PERCENTAGES OF GDP

Agriculture: 20.1; industry: 26.6; services: 53.3 (2017 estimate)

POPULATION BELOW POVERTY LINE

46.3 percent (2015 estimate)

EXPORTS

$11.74 billion (2017 estimate)

MAIN EXPORT PARTNERS

Netherlands: 11.8 percent; US: 7.9 percent; France: 6.4 percent; Belgium: 6.4 percent (2017)

MAIN EXPORTS

Coffee, cocoa, timber, petroleum, bananas, cotton, pineapples, palm oil, fish

MAIN IMPORT PARTNERS

Nigeria: 15 percent; France: 13.4 percent; China: 11.3 percent; US: 4.3 percent (2017)

MAIN IMPORTS

Fuel, food, capital equipment

CULTURAL CÔTE D'IVOIRE

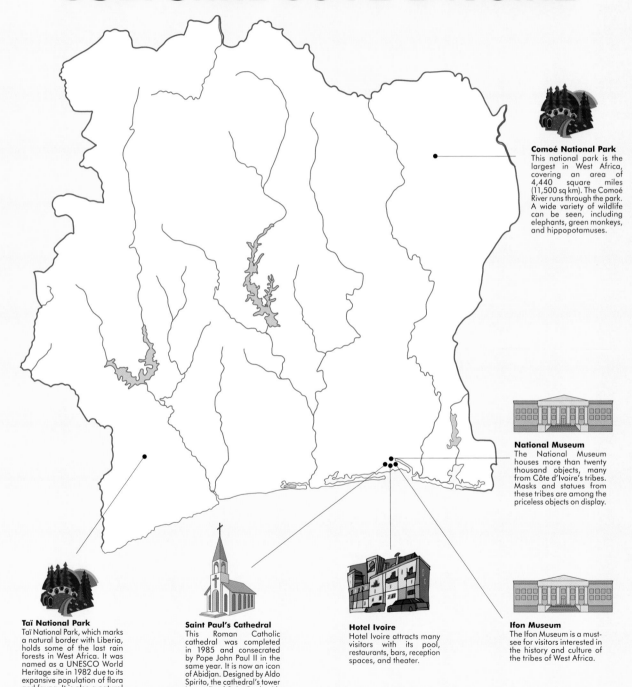

Comoé National Park
This national park is the largest in West Africa, covering an area of 4,440 square miles (11,500 sq km). The Comoé River runs through the park. A wide variety of wildlife can be seen, including elephants, green monkeys, and hippopotamuses.

National Museum
The National Museum houses more than twenty thousand objects, many from Côte d'Ivoire's tribes. Masks and statues from these tribes are among the priceless objects on display.

Taï National Park
Taï National Park, which marks a natural border with Liberia, holds some of the last rain forests in West Africa. It was named as a UNESCO World Heritage site in 1982 due to its expansive population of flora and fauna. It is also a natural reservoir for the Ebola virus.

Saint Paul's Cathedral
This Roman Catholic cathedral was completed in 1985 and consecrated by Pope John Paul II in the same year. It is now an icon of Abidjan. Designed by Aldo Spirito, the cathedral's tower is a stylized Saint Paul, with his robes trailing behind him.

Hotel Ivoire
Hotel Ivoire attracts many visitors with its pool, restaurants, bars, reception spaces, and theater.

Ifon Museum
The Ifon Museum is a must-see for visitors interested in the history and culture of the tribes of West Africa.

ABOUT THE CULTURE

OFFICIAL NAME
République de Côte d'Ivoire

DATE OF INDEPENDENCE
August 7, 1960

NATIONAL FLAG
Three equal vertical bands of orange (hoist side), white, and green. Design based on the flag of France.

TOTAL AREA
124,504 square miles (322,463 sq km)

COASTLINE
320 miles (515 km)

CLIMATE
Tropical along coast, semiarid in far north

HIGHEST POINT
Mount Nimba (5,748 feet/1,752 m)

CAPITAL
Yamoussoukro

MAIN CITIES
Abidjan, Abobo, Bouaké, Daloa, Korhogo, Man, San-Pédro

PORTS AND HARBORS
Abidjan, Aboisso, Dabou, San-Pédro

POPULATION
26.3 million (July 2018 estimate)

LIFE EXPECTANCY
60.1 years (2018 estimate)

MAJOR LANGUAGES
French (official language), Dyula, Senufo, Anyi, Baule, Dan/Yakuba

MAJOR ETHNIC GROUPS
Akan: 28.8 percent; Gur: 16.1 percent; Northern Mande: 14.5 percent; Kru: 8.5 percent; Southern Mande: 6.9 percent; unspecified: 0.9 percent; non-Ivoirian: 42.3 percent (2014)

MAJOR RELIGIONS
Islam: 42.9 percent; Christianity: 33.9 percent; indigenous religions: 3.6 percent; other religion: 0.5 percent; none: 19.1 percent (2014 estimate)

PRESIDENTS
Félix Houphouët-Boigny (served as president 1960—1993)
Henri Konan Bédié (served as president 1993—1999)
Laurent Gbagbo (served as president 2000—2011)
Alassane Dramane Ouattara (president 2010—)

TIMELINE

IN CÔTE D'IVOIRE	IN THE WORLD
	323 BCE Alexander the Great's empire stretches from Greece to India.
	1206–1368 CE Genghis Khan unifies the Mongols and starts conquest of the world. At its height, the Mongol Empire under Kublai Khan stretches from China to Persia and parts of Europe and Russia.
late 1400s Portuguese establish trading settlements along the coast.	
	1789–1799 The French Revolution.
1893 Côte d'Ivoire becomes a French colony.	
1904 Côte d'Ivoire becomes part of the French Federation of West Africa.	**1914–1918** World War I.
1946 Félix Houphouët-Boigny founds the interterritorial African Democratic Rally and the Ivory Coast Democratic Party.	**1939–1945** World War II.
1958 Côte d'Ivoire becomes a republic.	
1960 France grants independence under nation's first president, Félix Houphouët-Boigny. He holds power until he dies in 1993.	**1986** Nuclear power disaster at Chernobyl in Ukraine.
1990 Houphouët-Boigny wins first multiparty presidential elections.	
1993 Henri Konan Bédié becomes president.	
1995 Bédié is reelected.	**1997** Hong Kong is returned to China.
1999 Mutinying soldiers topple the government. Brigadier General Robert Gueï takes power.	
2000 Laurent Gbagbo becomes president.	

IN CÔTE D'IVOIRE	IN THE WORLD
2003 President Gbagbo accepts peace deal. Military chiefs and rebels declare end of war.	**2003** War in Iraq begins.
2005 Economist Charles Konan Banny is nominated as prime minister by mediators.	**2005** Hurricane Katrina devastates the Gulf Coast of the United States.
2009 The International Monetary Fund agrees to write off $3 billion of $12.8 billion national debt. Presidential election date is reset for early 2010.	**2009** Outbreak of flu virus H1N1 causes world pandemic.
2010 After an election is finally held, President Gbagbo is sworn in despite arguments from the United Nations and other world leaders, sparking months of violent conflict.	**2010** A 7.0 magnitude earthquake rocks Haiti, killing tens of thousands of people.
2011 Gbagbo is arrested and Alassane Ouattara is sworn in as president. The Truth, Reconciliation, and Dialogue Commission is formed.	**2011** Osama bin Laden is killed.
2012 President Ouattara dissolves the government following a dispute over a new marriage law.	**2012** The Sandy Hook shooting occurs.
2013 The gold mining industry begins to take off.	**2013** Pope Francis is elected.
2014 The ban on diamond mining officially ends.	**2014** A deadly Ebola outbreak hits West Africa, especially Liberia.
2015 Presidential election is held and President Ouattara wins reelection.	
2016 Islamist militants attack a resort near Abidjan, killing nineteen people.	**2016** Historic Paris Agreement on Climate Change is signed.
2017 Continuous mutinies cause the government to pay soldiers bonuses.	**2017** UK activates Article 50, triggering an exit from the European Union.
	2018 Myanmar military leaders face charges of genocide.

GLOSSARY

anaya (a-NAI-ya)
Offering of food to the gods during the yam festival.

arrears
Debt that is overdue.

attiéké (AT-tee-eck-eh)
Grated cassava dish.

awale (a-WA-lay)
Ivorian board game, a variant of mancala, similar to backgammon.

divination
A supernatural means of seeking knowledge of the future.

Eid al-Fitr
Celebration of the breaking of the fast at the end of the Islamic month of Ramadan.

Evangelical
A global, transdenominational movement within Protestant Christianity that focuses on the Bible as ultimate authority, the redemptive sacrifice of Jesus Christ, and the need to be transformed through a personal "born-again" experience, among other characteristics.

gendarmerie
Branch of armed forces responsible for general law enforcement; a national police.

griot
Elite people entrusted with passing down oral tradition and cultural heritage to succeeding generations. Griots are historians, praise singers, and musical entertainers.

gris-gris
Necklace amulet believed to ward off evil.

Hadith
Collection of the Prophet Muhammad's sayings that supplements the Quran in guiding Muslims.

hajj
Muslim pilgrimage to Mecca.

marabous
Traditional religious leaders of the Senufo.

maquis (MA-kee)
Outdoor eating place for quick meals.

masquerade
An event in which participants wear costumes, especially ornate masks.

PDCI
Democratic Party of Côte d'Ivoire; the only political party in the country after independence until multiparty elections were allowed in 1990.

salat (sa-LAHT)
Muslim prayer.

scepter
A symbolic staff or wand carried by rulers.

zakat (za-KAHT)
Islamic obligation of giving alms.

FOR FURTHER INFORMATION

BOOKS

Bjorklund, Ruth. *Côte d'Ivoire*. New York: Scholastic, 2019.

Feauxzar, Papatia. *Fofky's Kitchen: Easy Ivorian Recipes for Traditional and Street Foods*. Dallas, TX: Djarabi Kitabs, 2018.

The Museum Reitberg. *African Masters: Art from the Ivory Coast*. Zurich, Switzerland: Scheidegger and Spiess, 2015.

Newell, Sasha. *The Modernity Bluff: Crime, Consumption, and Citizenship in Côte d'Ivoire*. Chicago: University of Chicago Press, 2012.

Sykes, Tom. *Ivory Coast*. Chalfont St. Peter, UK: Bradt Travel Guides, 2016

WEBSITES

African Studies Center. Côte d'Ivoire page. https://www.africa.upenn.edu/Country_Specific/Cote.html.

FIFA.com. https://www.fifa.com/associations/association=civ/index.html.

International Monetary Fund Côte d'Ivoire. https://www.imf.org/en/Countries/CIV.

Languages of the World: Côte d'Ivoire. https://www.ethnologue.com/country/CI.

Music of Côte d'Ivoire. http://www.afromix.org/html/musique/pays/cote-d-ivoire/index.en.html.

MUSIC

Cote d'Ivoire: Baule Vocal Music (CD). Smithsonian Folkways Recordings, 2014.

BIBLIOGRAPHY

ACCRA Declaration. Participants' Statement. ACCRA Declaration on Forest Law Compliance in West African Countries. http://illegal-logging.info/uploads/1_AccraDeclarationAug20E1.pdf.

Amnesty International. "Côte d'Ivoire: Amnesty International Appeal to All Parties." http://www.amnesty.org/en/library/asset/AFR31/007/2000/en/f8fe6dc5-faaf-4abc-a63f-4b2368e6575a/afr310072000en.pdf.

———. "UN Closes Ivory Coast Mission, Security Remains Fragile," June 30, 2017. https://www.reuters.com/article/us-ivorycoast-un-peacekeepers-idUSKBN19L1VK.

Bavier, Joe. "Women Take Leading Roles as Ivory Coast Emerges from Turmoil," March 7, 2016. https://www.reuters.com/article/us-womens-day-ivorycoast/women-take-leading-roles-as-ivory-coast-emerges-from-turmoil-idUSKCN0W91IL.

"Civil War Allows Rampant Illegal Logging." IRIN News, December 23, 2004. http://www.irinnews.org/report.aspx?reportid=52512.

"Côte d'Ivoire." Encyclopaedia Britannica. https://www.britannica.com/place/Cote-dIvoire.

"Côte d'Ivoire." Reporters Without Borders. https://rsf.org/en/cote-divoire.

"Côte d'Ivoire: Events of 2017." Human Rights Watch. https://www.hrw.org/world-report/2018/country-chapters/cote-divoire#.

"Côte d'Ivoire in Photos." TrekEarth. http://www.trekearth.com/gallery/Africa/Cote_dIvoire.

"Country Profile: Ivory Coast." BBC News. https://www.bbc.com/news/world-africa-13287216.

Cynn, Christine. *Prevention: Gender, Sexuality, HIV, and the Media in Côte d'Ivoire.* Columbus, OH: Ohio State University Press, 2018.

District of Yamoussoukro. "Economic Perspectives." http://yamoussoukro.org.

Fall, Madio, and Souleymane Coulibaly. *Diversified Urbanization: The Case of Côte d'Ivoire.* Washington, DC: World Bank Publications, 2017.

"Ivory Coast's Gold Rush Comes at a Price." CNN, September 1, 2016. https://www.cnn.com/2016/09/01/africa/gallery/ivory-coast-gold-mpa/index.html.

Koua, Blaise K., Paul Magloire E. Koffi, Prosper Gbaha, and Siaka Touré. "Present Status and Overview of Potential of Renewable Energy in Côte d'Ivoire." *Renewable and Sustainable Energy Reviews* 41 (January 2015): 907—914.

Lonely Planet West Africa. Victoria, Australia: Lonely Planet, 2017.

Sullivan, Tara. *The Bitter Side of Sweet.* London, UK: Penguin Books, 2017.

UN Security Council. "Political Agreement Signed in March Eased Tensions in Côte d'Ivoire, but Delays in Implementation Growing Concern, Security Council Told." Relief Web, October 22, 2007. http://www.reliefweb.int/rw/rwb.nsf/db900sid/EGUA-788S8A?OpenDocument

"US Relations with Côte d'Ivoire." US Department of State, December 4, 2018. http://www.state.gov/r/pa/ei/bgn/2846.htm.

Vaughan, Julia Anne, and Ken Vaughan. *No Regrets: Caught in the Crossfire of an African Civil War.* Flagstaff, AZ: Morton Moore Publishing, 2017.

INDEX

Abidjan, 7, 10, 15—16, 24—25, 28, 34, 37, 39, 47, 49, 53—54, 62, 71, 73, 77, 79—81, 88—89, 96, 106, 109, 113—114, 118, 127
air travel, 53

bananas, 5, 22, 49, 51, 58, 67, 81, 126
Basilica of Our Lady of Peace, 15, 84, 88—89
beaches, 7, 10, 16—17, 51, 63, 111, 113
Bédié, Henri Konan, 25, 33, 36
biodiversity, 12, 17, 57—58, 61
Bouaké, 16, 73, 77, 79—81, 114
Burkina Faso, 5, 9, 27, 29, 33, 36, 48—49, 51, 66, 68, 70, 94, 128

cabinet, 32, 34, 71
cassava, 49, 122—126
cell phones, 52, 97, 113
child soldiers, 41
churches, 15, 88—89
civil wars, 19, 41, 51, 70, 77, 87, 100
    First Ivorian Civil War, 6, 14, 26—27, 33, 37—39, 51, 59—60, 69, 81
    Second Ivorian Civil War, 6, 28, 33—34, 36—38, 41—42, 60, 62, 77, 80, 89, 96
clans, 20, 67—68, 74, 80, 120
climate, 11—12
climate change, 49, 53, 57—58
clothing, 79, 120
cocoa, 5, 14—16, 23—24, 46, 48—49, 51, 58, 67, 75
coffee, 5, 15—16, 22—24, 46, 48, 50—51, 58
communications, 52—53, 96—97
conscription, 22
constitution, 25, 31, 34—36, 39—41, 85, 95
coup, 6, 26
crafts, 68, 99—103 107—108, 121
currency, 44, 52

Dadié, Bernard, 108
dams, 11, 13, 53
dance, 68, 100—104, 106—109, 111—112, 114, 119—121
debt, 25, 46, 80
deforestation, 10, 14, 17, 57—60, 73
diaspora, 19, 96—97, 104
divination, 90, 100
domestic violence, 40—41
drinks, 126—127
Duékoué Massacre, 28

ECOWAS, 26, 39
education, 16, 22, 43, 47—48, 54, 67—69, 71, 73—77, 88, 94—95, 106, 109, 112
elections, 6, 23, 25—28, 32—37, 40, 46
electricity, 13, 46, 48—49, 53—54
exports, 5—6, 14—15, 17, 22—24, 46—51, 54, 58—59, 61

family, 65, 69, 73—76, 78—81, 90
farming, 5, 10, 14—17, 22—23, 45—49, 54, 57—59, 61, 67—69, 73—75, 81, 90, 119—120, 124—126, 128
fishing, 13, 15, 69
food, 19—20, 49, 51, 59, 65, 69, 78, 118, 123—129
forced labor, 22—23, 41
foreign investment, 6, 46, 50—51, 53, 80
forests, 7, 9—14, 16—17, 58—61
France, 5—7, 15—16, 19, 21—24, 26, 34, 38—39, 42, 50—52, 70, 77, 89, 96—97, 100, 103—104, 108, 127, 129
free expression, 24, 39—40

games, 111—112
Gbagbo, Laurent, 25—28, 33—34, 37—38, 41—42, 128
Gbagbo, Simone, 42
gendarmerie, 39, 55

Ghana, 5, 9, 12, 20—21, 24, 28, 48—49, 54, 67—68, 70, 88, 94
gold, 20, 46—48, 51, 120
Grand-Bassam, 16, 18, 29, 85, 91, 111
greetings, 78
griot, 105
gris-gris, 90
Gueï, Robert, 26
Guinea, 5, 9, 67—68, 70, 82

Harris, William, 88
health care, 22, 42—43, 48, 67, 69, 71, 73, 80—83
highest point, 10
HIV/AIDS, 43, 75, 82—83
holidays and festivals
    Christmas, 117, 121
    Eid al-Fitr, 118
    Festival of Dipri, 118—119
    Festival of Masks, 119
    Ramadan, 86, 117—118
    yam festivals, 119—120
Houphouët-Boigny, Félix, 13, 19, 23—26, 33, 42, 88—89
housing, 69—71, 80—81
human trafficking, 41

imports, 49, 51, 54
independence, 5, 14—15, 19, 22—24, 31—32, 36, 42, 58, 75, 93, 109
International Criminal Court, 28, 42
International Monetary Fund, 25, 33, 46, 80
internet, 52—53, 96—97, 113
ivory, 5, 20, 99, 101

judiciary, 34, 40

Korhogo (city), 17, 81
korhogo cloth, 107—108

labor code, 55
lagoons, 10, 15, 51

INDEX

languages
French, 7, 54, 93—96
Gur/Senfo group, 94
Kru group, 93—94
Kwa group, 94
Mande group, 94—95
legislature, 24—26, 28—29, 31—35, 37, 39
LGBTQ community, 41, 70
Liberia, 5, 9, 21, 41, 66, 69—70, 82, 88, 94
literacy, 75, 77, 80, 95
literature, 95, 107—109
local government, 32

Mali, 5, 9, 29, 49, 51, 66, 68, 70, 94
Man (city), 17, 119
manufacturing, 48—50
maquis, 125, 127—128
marabous, 90
markets, 16, 67—68, 74, 125, 129
marriage, 28, 41, 67, 79, 104—105
masks, 68, 99, 101—103, 107, 119
masquerade, 101—103, 119
military, 24—29, 34, 37—40
Millennium Challenge Corporation, 43, 47—48
minimum wage, 54
missionaries, 21, 70, 88—89
mosques, 86—87, 118, 121
mountains, 9—11, 17
museums, 7, 16, 99—100, 103, 109
music, 93, 100, 102—107, 112, 119
mutinies, 25, 29, 38, 40

national parks, 10—11, 14, 17, 61, 114
natural gas, 49, 54
newspapers, 24—25, 95—96

oil, 49, 63
Ouattara, Alassane Dramane, 7, 25—29, 31—37, 39, 42—43, 46, 60—61, 83

palm oil, 5, 17, 24, 46, 51, 58, 80, 125—126

people
Abe (Abbey), 22
Abidji, 118
Abron, 10, 67—68, 120
Anyi (Agni), 10, 22, 67—68, 88, 90—91, 94, 119
Baule, 10, 22—23, 65, 67, 90—91, 94, 100, 102, 119
Dan (Yakuba), 68, 90, 94, 100, 102, 120
Dyula, 33, 67—68, 90, 94
French, 5, 16, 19, 21—24, 38—39, 70, 88, 100
Kru, 66, 69—70, 90, 93—94
Kulango, 69, 91, 94, 120
Lobi, 66, 68—69, 90, 94
Portuguese, 20—21, 123
Senufo, 66, 68, 81, 90, 94, 100, 102, 107
plant life, 10—12, 14, 58, 61
political parties
Democratic Party of Côte d'Ivoire (PDCI), 23—24, 32, 37
Ivorian Popular Front (FPI), 25
Rally of Republicans (RDR), 33, 36—37
pollution, 58, 62—63
population, 7, 13, 16, 58, 65—67, 73, 79—80, 88, 114
poverty, 14, 46—47, 54, 60, 71, 73, 80
press freedom, 24, 39—40, 95—96
protests, 6, 24—25, 28, 33, 40, 128

radio, 39, 96
railroads, 15—16
recipes, 130—131
refugees, 69
religion
Christianity, 6—7, 20—21, 79, 85—86, 88—89, 91, 96, 117, 121
Islam, 6—7, 20, 25—26, 29, 33, 68, 85—87, 91, 117—118
traditional beliefs, 67—68, 86—87, 89—91, 101—104, 118—120
renewable energy, 13, 53—54

rivers, 11—13, 61
roads, 15—16, 47, 52, 62

Saharan trade routes, 20, 100
sanctions, 27, 51
San-Pédro, 17, 53
savanna, 9—13, 16, 105
shekere, 102
slavery, 16, 20—21
slums, 80
Soro, Guillaume, 27, 35
sports, 111—115
storytelling, 70, 76, 95, 105, 112

taxes, 22, 128
television, 39—40
terrorism, 29, 51, 85, 91
textiles, 15—16, 20, 48—49, 99, 107—109
timber, 13—15, 17, 49—51, 58—61
tourism, 7, 16, 51, 63, 113—114, 125, 127
toxic waste, 62—63

United Nations, 6, 21, 26—28, 39—42, 51, 62, 69, 82, 96, 128
United States, 21, 32, 38, 42—43, 50—51, 70, 89, 105—106, 127
urbanization, 16, 54, 73, 78—80

video games, 97, 113, 115

wildlife, 7, 10—14, 51, 58, 61
women, 35, 41, 59, 66—67, 69, 74—75, 77—79, 81, 83, 87, 108, 123
World Bank, 34, 46, 49, 60—61, 80
World War I, 22
World War II, 23

Yamoussoukro, 7, 13, 15—16, 28, 38, 73, 77, 88—89, 113—114
yams, 16, 67, 69, 81, 91, 119—120, 125—126